This book is dedicated to the
fathers, brothers, boyfriends, and
husbands who don't lie.

To the ones who keep women believing
that not all men are dogs.

CONTENTS

INTRODUCTION

This is a book for girls who like boys.
We should know—we're two of them! And we want to help you keep liking boys.

So before we go any further, let's make one thing clear. Don't let the title of this book confuse you: It is *not* a manifesto against guys. And it's not a license to man-bash or blame a problem with one boy on an entire gender at large. If you came here looking to hate, move along.

What this book is, then, is a handbook for smart girls who are ready to deal with some of the messy truths about guys and relationships. If that's you, then listen up. Because we're going to get real with you—fast.

If you want to have a good relationship with guys, you need to question every word that comes out of their mouths.

Yes, it sounds harsh. But when it comes to getting what they want sexually, young men will say anything—literally *anything*—to make it happen. Seriously, a straight guy will profess to loving the Jonas Brothers if it helps him get in your pants.

We're not saying all guys are like this 100 percent of the time. Nor do they "only want one thing from you," as dads across the country have preached for generations. In fact, a lot of great guys say plenty of nice things to make girls feel genuinely pretty, sexy, worthwhile, and loved. Who can blame you for believing them or just wanting to get into their pants, too? Everyone is curious about what it's like to connect with the opposite sex, emotionally and physically. You won't see us making the mistake of assuming that you don't want sex just as much as guys do!

At the same time, there's usually a lot more at stake for girls when they do have sex. Young women are more likely to be the ones who end up brokenhearted, losing their self-respect, and even being physically or emotionally abused. It's not like guys are out to hurt girls. It's just that the inexperienced ones are often victims of their own urges. They want something—unlimited booty whenever and from whomever—and they're afraid the truth won't get it for them. Because if they admit that they might want to be with a girl just for sex, what kind of self-respecting gal would tolerate that? Eventually, boys get savvy and realize that the easiest way to get what they "need" is to distort the truth.

Being a smart girl, you can already spot a lot of the whoppers guys tell. You know—dumb, sexist stuff like "Chicks are dumber than guys" or "Bros before hos!" that they punctuate by high-fiving their buddies . . . which makes you want to high-five their faces. It's obvious that saying something so stupid, cruel, or outrageous can only be to get a rise out of you. Or because they're a few IQ points shy of human-being status.

But often, the most damaging things that guys say to gain control, power, or an ego boost are way more subtle. Like lies about your bodies, how sex should feel, and what gals owe guys physically and emotionally. They're also a lot harder to spot because you hear them during your most intimate moments with a boy.

They can come when one of you is feeling vulnerable (e.g., when he senses you're about to break up with him or are down on yourself) or even when you're feeling safe (e.g., when you have the upper hand in the relationship, or are cuddling up in his bed after a super fun party you both enjoyed). It's in these moments, when your guard is down and your heart is open, that you're most at risk.

So we thought it was time someone exposed why guys lie, the ways they do it, and how you can protect yourself. Through our interviews with hundreds of guys and some of the biggest relationship experts in psychology and sexuality, we've put together a list of 17 of the most common lies you and your friends will hear at some point in your lives.

Guys' lies run the gamut from innocuous to dangerous, with just about everything that's inappropriate, disgusting, insulting, and generally slap-your-forehead wrong in between. Sadly, a lot of them may be familiar to you. Discovering that someone you care about told you one of these things just to get something from you or even to hurt you really sucks. But it blows even more to keep believing that lie when you're on the verge of doing some not-so-smart things with your body and heart just to get close to a guy.

This book will help you identify a lie when you hear it and figure out who to trust. But in a larger way, it helps you sharpen your instincts and safeguard yourself from people who don't have your best interests at heart. Have you ever heard the phrase *caveat emptor*? It's Latin, and it translates roughly into "buyer beware." Basically, it's something that people say before you plunk down anything of value in exchange for something another person is selling. It's a caution to do your research, figure out what's motivating the seller, and be aware that everyone has an agenda.

You probably do this all the time when a salesperson persuades you to buy a lip gloss or a cute outfit. Ideally, she'll be honest about how it really looks on you. But she's got an interest in closing the deal—it helps her earn a commission and makes her company more money. You can look in the mirror and try to figure out if that shade or shape really flatters you. But it's hard to be objective when she's whispering in your ear, "Oh my God, that is so you!"

Before you buy a boy's spiel about sex and romance, it's important to know what's motivating him and what's the *real* agenda behind what he's telling you. Being skeptical isn't bitchy. It's brilliant, because if you don't let guys play you for a fool, you can't get played, period. And once you know the truth and stand up for it, you start attracting the better kinds of guys: the ones who *want* you to teach them how girls deserve be treated. Even though they may seem clueless and crass on the surface, most boys really do crave education on how to be with (and be good to) strong, smart, and secure young women.

How to Use This Book

Here's how it works: Each chapter lays out one lie, with some variations on the same theme, that guys might tell you. Then we explain the truth, backed up with scientific proof, expert opinions, and real-life experiences from girls and guys.

You should know upfront that some issues we tackle aren't as black and white as we'd like. We don't expect you to agree with everything we say. In a way, we hope you don't. Though it's all based on the best research and advice we could find, the information might differ from what your family and friends believe, especially when it comes to controversial issues like teen pregnancy and homosexuality. That's okay. The point is to get you thinking independently about what you believe, depending on your personal circumstances and experiences. We hope it encourages you to start your own fact-finding mission and figure out what's right for you. You might not have faced some of these issues yet, but odds are you or a friend soon will. It's important to have a plan so you don't end up convincing yourself that something harmful to you may be okay after all.

After we lay out the facts, we give some options of things to say back to any guy to refute the lie and start a more truthful dialogue. They range from goody-two-shoes earnest to holy-crap-that-girl-is-fierce sassy—hopefully you will find something in between that sounds like you, that feels right in the moment. What's most important is that you say *something*. We recommend you practice these phrases in your own ways—to your BFF or just your mirror—before you need to use them. The more comfortable you get saying them, the better you can stick to your guns and not get dissuaded by his cute puppy-dog eyes or intimidating threat.

Even if you've already bought the lie—maybe you did something sexually you didn't want to in the past, or you let bad behavior slide because you weren't sure it was wrong—we'll let you know exactly what to do to right the situation. Ideally, it'll make a guy start backpedaling as if it's an Olympic sport. And if he doesn't, you'll have the confidence to exit the situation feeling mentally, physically, and emotionally stronger than ever.

We've also included Q&As based on our interviews with hundreds of teen girls and young women and what they think is need-to-know info about relationships and sex. We hope these questions get to the heart of what's on your mind, no matter how embarrassing or whacked-out they seem. Please know that all of the questions are totally normal, and actually rather common. We guarantee that the weirdest thing you've ever wondered about is something that millions of girls before you have secretly pondered, too.

At this point you probably have a few questions for us. We know we would. So we'll try to tackle them for you.

What Makes You the Experts on Guys?

If you read our resumés, you'll find out that one of us (Belisa) is a clinical psychologist who has had extensive training in adolescent psychology and years of experience counseling young women in mental, emotional, and sexual health issues. She's written other books about depression, self-help, and dating, and you might even have seen her on one of the morning shows talking about the psychological side of current events.

The other coauthor (Holly) is a magazine writer and editor; most recently the features editor of *Cosmopolitan* and *Seventeen* magazines. You might have read her stories about guy behavior, sex, friendships, relationships, careers, even celebrities, in your favorite magazines. She also wrote a book for the Girl Scouts of the USA about body image and beauty.

Between us, we have a few decades of experience working with the top experts in psychology and male behavior. In addition to all of this, we've been in your shoes. Though we're a little older than you—okay, maybe a lot older—we still totally get the special role that guys play in your life. We're both single, and we're still in love with the way guys can make us burst out laughing or shake our heads in disgust, turn us on like nobody's business, make us spend hours awake at night analyzing their behavior, and generally frustrate the hell out of us. Not a lot of other sex educators—especially the pointy-headed academics in lab coats—can say the same thing.

Because we spend so much time with teens, we know that when your heart throbs for a cute guy, you end up doing a lot of crazy things. Like pretending to be into a band that makes your ears bleed just because he likes it. (Exhibit A for us? Hoobastank. Never again, ladies, never again.) Or following a guy to his college, even though it's way below the caliber of the one that accepted you. And don't even get us started on the sappy letters you write him, full of poetry so bad it would embarrass a third-grader.

Most of these mistakes can be reversed. You delete the bad tunes from your iPod. You transfer schools. You buy the letters off your ex before they can become blackmail material.

But some of the stuff you do because a guy tells you to can have enormous consequences. Not just the obvious ones, like getting pregnant or catching a sexually transmitted infection (STI) from having unprotected sex. We're talking long-term implications: how you define your sexuality, what you expect and tolerate from men, and how you view your body. These things aren't apparent at the moment you accept a guy's lies. But they help construct a pattern for relationships that lasts the rest of your life. Put yourself in positive, forward motion from the beginning, and you're pretty much set. Get hurt, sidetracked, or abused early on, and it's much harder to find or even recognize healthy relationships later. Not to mention you could miss out on some of the best experiences with boys that you'll have in your life if you get caught up hating one guy.

That's why we're making it our mission to get you started on the right track so you have plenty of time to discover and appreciate all the incredible things guys have to offer when you're in a healthy partnership.

One of My Parents Gave This Book to Me. WTF?

So they've officially creeped you out. We can't be sure of their exact reasons for putting this in your hands, but we're pretty sure of this: They care about you. And they are fuh-reaking out right now.

As chaotic as this stage in your life is, it's a weird time for them, too. They're thinking back to how they felt when they were your age. As they watch you deal with guys and sex for the first time, memories of their own teen years come flooding back, as vivid as if they had happened only yesterday. And they can't help but worry how your experience compares to theirs. So they start stressing for one of four reasons:

1 They did some crazy stuff they do *not* want you to know about. Remember, they're supposed to be authority figures in your life. Not the crazy partier who got trashed at the prom and passed out half naked on her own parents' lawn the morning after. Some of the stuff that happened may have hurt them—or someone else—emotionally or physically. Part of them fears you'll go down the same path.

2 They had a great time in their teens. Supportive friends, awesome dating experiences, and a loving family—the whole, happy ball of wax. They'll try their best to provide you with that last part, but they're anxious that your experience with the first two can't possibly measure up.

3 They were sexually inexperienced. Maybe they didn't lose their V-card until their 20s, so they can't relate to a

daughter who matures much earlier than they did. By the way, based on what most parents hear in the media and see in our sex-crazed culture, a lot of them assume that every kid is a raging nympho compared to what they were like.

4 They can't even remember what it was like to be a teen. This is the least common scenario—most adults are actively trying to forget their adolescence. But it does happen. Whether they're just too consumed with adult responsibilities or it wasn't that big a deal to them, this hazy memory can make a parent feel scarily out of touch with their kid.

All this accounts for why they'd rather you just stay the baby girl they've been used to for the last decade or so. They know that's not an option, but that won't stop them from doing dumb stuff if they think it'll help. Like telling a few cautionary tales of their own youth that are way, *way* too TMI. Or becoming superstrict, making your curfew much harsher than anyone else's . . . even though your rep is lily-white compared to the other girls you know. Or clamming up altogether, never saying one word to you about guys or sex.

Any of those reactions can weird you out, make you feel judged, abandoned, or totally misunderstood. But know this: The last thing in the world they want is to hurt you or see you get hurt by someone else. They just know that for you learn how to protect your heart, it probably has to get broken first. That's not easy to admit, and even harder to talk about with the one person you love most. But since this book is in your hands, it's a sign that they're eager to try.

We hope what you read here can be a great jumping-off point for some honest conversations with your parents. You'd better accept right now that it's going to be awkward. But cut them some slack and try to be open. It's the best gift you can give Mom and Dad to repay them for all that love they've given you.

So Now What?

Time to dig in! We know you have so much going on in your day, and we're grateful you're spending some of it with us. Our only request is that when you read this book, try to press the pause button on life for a minute. Turn off your computer. Put your cell on silent. Forget about what you heard at school today or the last thing the guy you like told you. Focus on who *you* are. And get ready to become the ultimate BS detector.

A Parent's Guide to *Boys Lie*

So you're the mom or dad of a teen girl. One who you think is kind of, maybe, possibly, verging on *considering* being sexually active. Welcome to the jungle.

There are a lot of things you're going through right now that your daughter simply isn't going to understand. Like how you wish you could fast-forward through the achingly awkward years ahead to the happily-ever-after part of your daughter's life where she's in a stable, supportive relationship with someone who adores her. Or maybe rewind to a few years back when she was an innocent kid whose only concern about guys was how to kick their butt on the soccer field.

Of course, reality can't be DVR'd like that. And some important truths about what she's going through now can't be saved for later. Chiefly these:

- Your daughter *will* have sex, soon, if she hasn't already. Maybe even with a guy or two you can't stand.

- Your daughter *will* have her heart broken. Probably by some creep who doesn't deserve to breathe the same air as she.
- Your daughter *will* be exposed to scary realities like pregnancy, sexually transmitted infections (STIs), and dating violence. If not directly, then through friends and peers, many of whom may scare the living daylights out of you.

Before you reach for a paper bag, read this: Your daughter *will* end up okay. Because she has a parent who's offering her the truth about sex, without judgment.

At least that's what we surmise if you're letting her check out *Boys Lie*. What you should know up front is that this isn't your conventional teen sex guide. But then there's nothing traditional about the world your daughter is living in right now. Guides on how to "survive" their teen years with their virginity hermetically sealed no longer apply. What teen girls require is guidance on how to preserve their integrity, self-respect, health, and sanity in an age of technology addiction, mixed messages, and hookups without heart.

Why Your Daughter Needs This Book . . . And You Do, Too

Since she was born, you knew that it would be hard to connect with your kid during her teen years. You just didn't know that she'd come of age in the midst of a total moral apocalypse of sexting, pregnancy pacts, and celebrity sex tapes. Or that you'd be competing with its four horsewomen—Britney Spears, Paris Hilton, Lindsay Lohan, and Kim Kardashian—for some air time.

Your daughter's most turbulent years just happen to coincide with a particularly conflicted culture when it comes to sex. Its message to young women: Be sexy yet sexless. Express your "girl power" with a midriff-bearing, bedazzled "SLUT" T-shirt. Work hard, and you can be anything—or just flash your rack on a reality show and . . . poof, you get your own line of handbags and perfume!

No wonder teen girls are walking cauldrons of contradictions. They appear more sophisticated at 12 than you were at 22. But though their bodies and attitudes are adult-like, their minds and emotions haven't caught up yet. And that results in a real naiveté about how their actions, especially boy-related ones, can impact their lives well after adolescence.

Our Approach to Sex and Sensibility

No matter how much parents panic about kids experimenting with their bodies and emotions, treating teen sexuality like a ticking time bomb they need to be shielded from doesn't help. It'll still blow up in your face eventually.

Instead, we prefer that you as a parent approach sex education as if you were bestowing the keys to a hot car to your daughter. You both recognize it has head-turning value. Part of the fun is showing it off, even making people envious of the person in the driver's seat. But for all the thrills it can unleash, there are equally serious consequences if it's not treated with respect. What happens if she takes it faster than she should or drives it under the influence? And what could result if she hands over the keys to just anyone? You never know if it could come back in even better condition—or twisted beyond recognition.

This book is part owner's manual—focusing on the body and the parts inside that make it run—and part street map. We hope to encourage your daughter to get to know her sexuality, where she wants to go with it, and to choose the safest road to get there.

A few other things you should know:

- **We don't hate guys.** Just the idea that girls are supposed to validate themselves through them. Some boys prey on this vulnerability, which is why girls end up believing lies like, "I'll pull out before I come" or "Have a drink, sex will feel better." Lots of the lies we lay out might seem obvious to you, but when the approval of a guy is at stake, any girl can rationalize away good sense.

  What we're hoping to prevent with *Boys Lie* is the misconception that the bad consequences of sex are all the boys' fault and solely the girls' responsibility. But until guys shoulder more of the physical and social burdens—like unwanted pregnancy—expect a whole mess of trouble if we don't empower young women to protect themselves.

- **We don't promote an abstinence-only agenda.** In a perfect world, kids would stay celibate until they find a partner who honors and respects them for life. That isn't happening. More than two of every three American teens have sexual intercourse before age 19, and they're having risky, unprotected sex younger than ever, many as early as age 12.

  When we focus exclusively on saying *no* to sex, we shut out a huge population of teens who have already said *yes*— almost half of kids nationwide. They desperately need advice about the challenges they're facing, like correct condom usage, limiting their number of sex partners, and avoiding sex with people who do have many other sex partners. Ignore the advice and the result is inexcusably high rates of unwanted pregnancies (currently more than 750,000 teens become pregnant in the U.S. each year) and STIs (one in four teen girls).

A common concern is that if you level with your daughter about sex, it's like rubber-stamping promiscuity. But studies on comprehensive sex education, which promotes delaying sex as long as possible and teaches safer sex techniques for those who are already having sex, document that this isn't the case. Comprehensive sex education actually helps lower risky sexual behavior, boosts condom use, and cuts the transmission of HIV among teens.

Also, if your daughter is among those seeking information and guidance, she's going to find it one way or another. Would you rather the truth come from a sleazy guy who convinces her unprotected sex is really as mind-blowing as everyone says it is? Because it's one thing to know what size and technique to use when it comes to condom use. It's quite another thing to know how to convince yourself and your partner that it's the *right* thing to do when every nerve in your body is telling you how it would feel amazing to go without one. That's what we hope to teach from a no-nonsense, compassionate, and shame-free angle.

- **We'll deal with some uncomfortable sexual information in explicit terms.** It's all but guaranteed you'll shift awkwardly in your seat, blush, or bolt for the nearest exit at some point. While we won't advocate having anal sex or threesomes, we can't ignore that some girls are doing just that. Or at least talking about it.

Unless we address extreme sex acts in the frank terms they themselves use, young people won't take seriously the risks associated with them. Statistics don't help—they hit home with your daughter about as well as the "Chlamydia is not a flower" filmstrips did when you were in school. Nor will sermons or scare tactics, especially coming from parents who "couldn't possibly understand what teen life is *really* like."

- **We are experts.** One of us (Belisa) is a clinical psychologist, who has worked in hospitals and private practice for over 20 years, and who speaks with women about relationships every day; and the other (Holly) is the former features editor of *Seventeen* and *Cosmopolitan* magazines and author of a book for teen girls on self-esteem and body image.

We're also single women dating in New York City who are all too familiar with how players operate. Since we're not the ones who need to shield her from them like you do, we can level with her without worrying that she'll kill or tune out the messenger. If you're not the one lecturing, it frees you to have a more meaningful follow-up conversation with her about sex and relationships. One, we hope, that won't involve quite as much eye rolling or "Why can't you just leave me alone and be normal for once?" sass as it might otherwise.

The Morning After: What the Heck to Do Once Your Daughter Reads This

On the list of things you'd rather not do, having a sex talk with your kid probably ranks up there with fighting a grizzly bear. On top of an erupting volcano. During an F-5 tornado. While you're buck-naked.

But whatever your moral or religious stance on teen sex, we encourage you not to hide your daughter from reality just to make yourself feel comfortable. (Consider what happens when she finds out you lied about sex and that it actually *is* fun and not something only for adults. What else will she think you're not telling the truth about?) And you can't leave sex talk to schools. It may never happen there, or it may come too late.

Raising a sexually responsible teen requires a continuing dialogue about sex and relationships. Not just a one-time chat on her thirteenth birthday. It should happen every time there's yet another sex scandal regarding a politician or sports figure. Or when a girl at her school is forced to drop out because of an unintended pregnancy. Or as the three-month anniversary with her new boyfriend approaches. Here's how to get the dialogue started.

1 **Keep the lines of communication open.** More than 40 percent of adolescents have intercourse before talking to their parents about safe sex, birth control, or sexually transmitted diseases. Scary, huh? Your daughter may be afraid you'll turn your back on her, or be disappointed to know what she's up to. She may even lie to you about what she's doing and compromise her health as a result. (Case in point: One survey asked underage teens who came to a Planned Parenthood center in Wisconsin seeking sexual healthcare services what they would do if they had to tell their parents they were using contraceptives. The majority said they would stop going to the clinic or quit using any sexual health-care service. Only 1 percent said

they would stop having sexual intercourse.)

The more willing a girl is to tell a parent about her experience with risky behaviors, the more likely she is to actually *avoid* doing them. Position yourself as a sounding board she can trust. That may mean doing more listening than talking at first. But you do need to spell it out that when she shares with you, you're not going to fly off the handle or lose respect for her. Your relationship is a safe space for honesty.

When she does ask your opinion, tell her where you're coming from regarding the following issues:

- What you know to be true in your family about love, respect, and intimacy.
- What sex and relationship lies you fell for once, whether it was from a member of the opposite sex, friends, or the media.
- What fears you have about your daughter and the stage she's at emotionally, sexually, and mentally.

It's hard to be honest, but in doing so, you may even win her respect and admiration for not babying her with half-truths. And if the only responses she gives you are huffs and sighs, it doesn't mean she's not listening. You may want to offer another trusted adult in whom she can confide, like an aunt, uncle, clergyperson, or family friend. It's not passing the buck; you are just reminding her that you're there for her, albeit indirectly.

2 **Know what you're up against.** Think you know what your kid is up to? You probably don't know the half of it. Studies have shown that parents generally underestimate their children's experiences with drug use, stress, depression, and sexual activity. Only a small number of parents, 22 percent, say they think their teenagers have become sexually active, with 75 percent saying their kids have put it off.

When it comes to sex, it's not that we're not paying attention. It's that we're paying attention to the wrong things. Each week there's a new salacious headline about a teen sex epidemic: jelly bracelets that telegraph how many sex partners a 13-year-old has had, or Internet predators who use Facebook to snatch pubescent girls.

But really, the chance of your girl becoming one of these headlines is pretty slim. They're just sensational red herrings, distracting you from a bigger story: the fact that your daughter could be turning into the next faceless pregnancy statistic or contracting a sexually transmitted infection right now. In your basement. With the sweet kid next door you've known since he wore Pull-Ups.

Unless you're taking the initiative to investigate what your daughter is reading, watching, and listening to, who she's texting and talking to online, and what the culture is like at her school, you won't know what's influencing her decisions. It isn't enough to know if she's into shows that glorify sex without contraception, consequences, or commitment. You have to ask questions about *why* she likes them so much, and what she and her friends think they say about what's the norm for kids her age.

Don't be afraid to be overbearing as long as you're doing it with compassion. (Caveat: Never bait siblings against one another to get intel unless you want to reenact the Civil War beneath your roof. There's no faster way to get a daughter to

resent you than asking her siblings to betray confidences.)
If you know what risky activities she may be up to, you can
come up with mutually satisfying ways to keep her safer.

3   **Be there for her.** Seems simplistic, but it works. If
you make home a welcoming place to be, she'll spend
more time there and avoid seeking affection from toxic
outside sources. Teens who participate in family activities—
like movie nights, sit-down dinners, and shopping trips—
are less likely to engage in risky sex activities.

In addition, research shows that parents who have warm
relationships with their children are better at helping their
kids understand their messages about sex and relationships.
Dads, this means you, too. When teens engage in risky sexual
behavior, there's a misconception that fathers are the first to
freak out and drop off the radar. Not true. Dads actually tend
to *up* their involvement in their children's lives, keeping tabs
on their friends and their behaviors, paying closer attention
to their schedules, and so on. A weekly coffee date or nose-
bleed seats to a ballgame can be critical, even if you don't say
much to each other. Those activities make it easier for her
come to you when she needs someone to raise her spirits as
she navigates a sea of jerks out there. Most of all, make your
own behavior a living reminder that there *are* good guys out
there. She'll believe it when she sees you're one of them.
(And it couldn't hurt to let her know that you'll take your
entire Craftsman tool set to the skull of any bad ones who
dare to mess with her.)

LIE #1

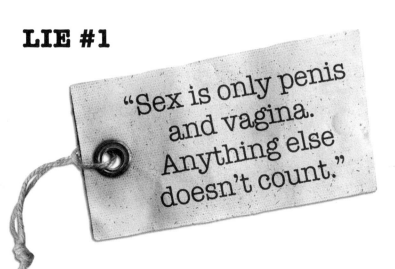

"Sex is only penis and vagina. Anything else doesn't count."

DEFINING SEX, VIRGINITY, AND WHAT YOU'RE REALLY DOING WHEN YOU HOOK UP

🐾 Other Ways He **MIGHT** Say It

- ✗ "We're not having sex, we're just fooling around."
- ✗ "Blow jobs aren't really sex."
- ✗ "We can do anal and you'll still be a virgin."
- ✗ "Just putting the tip in doesn't mean we've had sex."
- ✗ "If you don't tell anyone you've had sex, you're technically a virgin."

☞ The **TRUTH**:

S-E-X. Small word. **Ginormous** idea. You'd need a crowbar to cram any more importance, mystery, fun, danger, or confusion into three little letters.

Since the term "sex" was coined (in the 14th century, FYI), it's referred mostly to penis/vagina (P/V) intercourse between a man and a woman. Of course, a lot has changed in the 600-odd years since then. We still couple up for good ol' baby-making pene-tration; however, today it's less of an issue if the two people doing it haven't said "I do" yet. Or if they're the same sex. Or if there are actually more than two of them getting busy at once. Or if strangers are watching it all go down live via webcam or on a DVD.

It's easy to be blasé about how XXX-treme our world has become. Think about it: A new "leaked" tape of a celeb going down on her latest fling makes TMZ headlines for only a couple days. Then it's bumped aside by news of yet another professional athlete's or politician's affair.

What happens onscreen, even just on OMFG episodes of *Gossip Girl*, would surely shock the stockings off the guy who first uttered "sex" in the fourteenth century. Still, it might not qualify as "real" sex, if you're just going by the old P/V-only definition. And that makes a big difference when a guy tries to talk to you about sex and what he expects from you.

What Counts as Sex?

Health experts define sex as any of the following activities that take place between two people, regardless of gender:

1. Vaginal intercourse

2. Anal intercourse

3. Oral sex—both a person going down on you
   and you going down on him/her

4. Genital touching

Surprised? You thought it was only 1, right? Yeah, you and pretty much everyone else you know.

In fact, a new study from the Kinsey Institute for Research in Sex, Gender, and Reproduction reports that adults with plenty of booty experience under their belts aren't clear on what sex means either. The most shocking findings:

- About 30 percent of people do not consider oral sex to be "real sex."
- Approximately 20 percent of respondents think anal sex doesn't count as sex.
- Almost 89 percent of people don't consider vaginal intercourse as having sex if there is no ejaculation.

The truth is that sex really does go way beyond the guy/girl, penis/vagina you're used to. If it happens between a male and a female, between two females, between two males, whatever—all of the above count.

So why do so many people forget about or minimize everything that isn't vaginal intercourse? A lot of it has to do with the possibility of pregnancy. Many people, particularly those for whom religion is really important, think sex exists for the sole purpose of procreation. If there isn't a high possibility of popping out a kid nine months after you do the deed, it doesn't feel like the real thing. Like Christmas without snow. Diet instead of regular. *American Idol* after Paula left the show. Just not the genuine article.

So believing that only penis/vagina sex is "real" sex ignores some mammoth issues. First, you can still get off with #2–#4 on this sexual menu. Number two: believing that only #1 is "real" sex totally ignores the fact that, hello, there *is* a risk of getting pregnant if a guy slips his penis in the wrong hole during anal. Third, and most critical, you can pass on sexually transmitted infections (STIs) doing *all* of the above activities. In the case of oral and anal, the woman has an even greater chance of getting one than the man does, but she may not get as much pleasure from the activity.

Why on earth would women deny these truths and take on more physical burden than benefit? For a lot of girls, it boils down to one thing: Keeping their V-cards.

Saying only vaginal intercourse counts is pretty convenient for guys and girls who want to stay virgins until marriage but still get to know each other's bodies very intimately in the meantime. And that opens up a giant loophole that shady dudes often exploit to get a girl to go further sexually than she'd planned.

Some guys argue that a girl going down on them isn't "real"

sex. Same with letting them penetrate you anally or giving them a hand job. They make you feel almost stupid for thinking it's any more significant than putting on a pair of socks. *You can't get pregnant or lose your virginity from it. What's the big deal?*

The big deal is that those things can be just as intimate, even a lot less safe, than vaginal intercourse. If you don't use protection you can end up pregnant. You have a very real risk of getting an STI every time you do anything where your genitals or body fluids enter the equation.

Like a Virgin (but not quite)

According to one study, 11 percent of girls ages 15–17 said they'd had heterosexual oral sex but not vaginal intercourse. As a group, 16 percent of teenagers say they've had oral sex but haven't yet had intercourse.

Membership Has Its Privileges: What It Means to Carry Your V-Card

When we talk about virginity, there are only two options—you have it or you don't, no middle ground. And any time humans are faced with an either/or situation, our nature is to apply labels to each option. Bad, good. Dirty, clean. Spoiled, pure. Cool, loser.

It may make us feel better about our choices if the option we've chosen has a positive meaning. But sex is way too personal and complex to be described in one word. And your worth as a human being is completely unrelated to your sexual experience.

Being a good person has nothing to do with whether you've had sex or not; rather, it has to do with how you honor and respect yourself and other people. That's something that can only be proven by actions, not by some symbol or status. A purity ring doesn't guarantee the person wearing it is a good guy any more than a "Mom" tattoo ensures that its owner would really make a mother proud.

Unfortunately, many people use their virginity status to prove they're better or worse than someone else. (See "Virgins Out Loud" below). It's also used as a sexist tactic to weaken girls' power. Virginity is something that's "taken" by guys or "lost" like a set of car keys. Or it's a "gift" that girls save for the one person who can put a ring on their finger. That's not to say that virginity isn't a valuable thing. It is, if you want it to have meaning in your life. But it's not anyone else's business to judge or control.

Summer Lovin'
More Americans lose their virginity in June than in any other month. That's probably due to milestones that take place at this time like a prom and graduation, and simply having more time on your hands to fool around when school is out.

Virgins Out Loud

Is it okay to sell abstinence with sex? Some people have questioned whether it's right to look at this concept as something you buy and sell, but others are cashing in on it through iPhone apps that let you pledge to remain pure, and even underwear that announces you're proud to be a virgin.

The Candie's Foundation, an organization that promotes waiting to have sex (and whose latest spokesperson just happens to be teen mom Bristol Palin), got a lot of flak for selling revealing T-shirts that say, "I'm sexy enough to keep you waiting . . ." and "Be sexy. It doesn't mean you have to have sex." People questioned what the real message was on these tiny tanks: that girls who aren't sexy aren't worth the wait? Or that you can be a sexual object worth looking at, but you can't have the pleasure that sex involves?

We're all for dressing cute, but wouldn't it be better to voice your opinion on virginity, whatever that may be, with your mouth and not your chest? We encourage you to have a real conversation about sexuality without focusing on the body as much as on the mind and the heart.

The Sex Scale

WHATEVER YOU'VE DONE sexually in the past or want to do in the future, it's critical to understand each stage of sexual activity, from kissing to boning, and the impact it can have on your body. Here, we break down the need-to-know (NTK) info about each activity, from lowest risk to most dangerous. Pay super-close attention to each one's potential for pregnancy, STIs, and other health issues, and to how to stay safe if you choose to do them.

Kissing

NTK. This is the mouth-to-mouth connection you know and love. Any technique that involves putting your lips, tongue, and teeth together—whether it's pecking or sloppy necking—counts.

Risk factor. Very low for most sexually transmitted infections, and nil for pregnancy. STIs like HIV and hepatitis B and C aren't an issue in saliva, but if there is any blood in that saliva, then there is a risk of contracting an STI. But we're guessing you'll avoid sucking face with anyone who has bloody spit in the first place.

The one STI you do need to take into account when kissing is herpes. This can spread through skin-to-skin contact with an infected area or sore, and some people with this STI have sores on their mouths. Then again, other open sores look like herpes but can just be an infected pimple or a cold sore, which is caused by a strain of herpes that's totally different from the STI version and relatively harmless.

How to stay safe. Don't kiss a guy who has an open sore on his face or any blood in his saliva. You can ask whether it's a cold sore or a fever blister, but he may not know for sure so it's best to wait until it heals and he's been tested. Be even more careful if you have a cut on your mouth or recently had your tongue or lip pierced, as whatever he's got could go directly into your bloodstream.

Over the Clothes Touching and Rubbing

NTK. You might have heard this referred to in health class as "heavy petting." So 1950s, right? No actual pets are involved, except for you and your horndog guy pawing each other while fully clothed.

Risk factor. None for either STIs or pregnancy, as long as the skin is covered by a decently thick layer of clothing (nothing with holes or tissue-thin fabrics), and there is no skin-on-skin contact with genitals or bodily fluids.

How to stay safe. Keep fully clothed. Make sure any parts that have touched one person's bodily fluids (other than saliva) stay away from the other person's skin.

Dry Sex (AKA Dry Humping)

NTK. Not everyone agrees on the definition of this one. Also called outercourse, it can mean anything from acting out the motions of sex while you both stay fully clothed to getting naked and simulating intercourse. The dry part is a little mis-leading, since this type of foreplay can cause you to get very wet or lead a guy to ejaculate.

One thing that is agreed on: Humping and bumping of bodies together for pleasure at this stage means that the penis is never inserted into the vagina.

Risk factor. Low, if you both stay fully clothed. Even if he does come in his pants, the sperm can't swim through jeans. But the risk is higher for both STIs and pregnancy if one of you has exposed genitals and the other person is only semi-clothed. A thin layer of lacy underwear won't necessarily protect you if he ejaculates right outside your vulva.

If no clothes are on and you're exposed to each other's genitals or bodily fluids, there's a risk of getting an STI through skin-on-skin contact. And you absolutely can get pregnant if he comes just outside your vagina without penetrating you.

How to stay safe. Dry sex is actually a very slippery slope. Once you've stripped down, it's much harder than you think to keep your desires in check and avoid going all the way. Unless you're prepared to have protected sex with a condom if things get heated, it's better to keep your pants on and avoid the temptation to slide into home.

Mutual Masturbation

NTK. This refers to any time a guy touches, rubs, or strokes his penis as a girl does the same thing to her clitoris, nipples, or vulva, or inserts fingers in her vagina. This happens *without* the two people touching each other. For a relatively safe and fun activity, fewer couples do it then you'd think. It can be scary to be so exposed and vulnerable in front of another person. But if you're going to know how to please your partner, it helps to watch him "choke his chicken" (or her to "diddle" herself) long before you have vaginal sex. Oh, by the way, those old wives tales about masturbation causing acne or blindness? Complete crap.

Risk factor. None, as long as you're not touching each other. But you need to be careful about what happens with your bodily fluids. If he comes on a towel and then that towel touches your vulva, there is a risk of STIs and pregnancy.

How to stay safe. Keep your hands to yourself, but anywhere you like on your bod. If you are tempted to touch each other partway through, you'll need to have him put on a condom and to wash your hands thoroughly before doing this.

Genital Touching
(AKA Fingering and Hand Jobs)

NTK. This is when a guy touches your vulva, clitoris, inside your vagina, or your anus to stimulate you. Or you touch his penis, balls, or anus to do the same. If you're rubbing him, he may ask you to use lotion or lube, even baby powder, to cut down on friction. (Fun fact: It's also called digital sex, though there's no need for a computer.)

Risk factor. None for pregnancy, as long as neither one of you put any fingers (his or yours) near your V-zone after they've been handling his penis. STIs are a different story. Viruses and bacteria can get into the body through tiny cuts or tears in the skin. If you have a hangnail or blister on your hand and it comes into contact with his semen, you could get whatever infection he's carrying, even if he has no physical signs of it. And with herpes or genital warts (HPV), you don't even need to have a direct pathway to your bloodstream like a cut. You can get them simply from skin contact.

Also, if you let a guy touch your backdoor and then go to your vagina, he could transfer fecal matter that could cause a serious infection in your V-zone.

How to stay safe. To be totally protected, you should wear a latex glove or put a condom on any fingers that will touch each other's genitals. If you think this isn't practical for you, it's very important to avoid genital touching if you see or feel any bumps or sores on his genitals or if you have any open sores or cuts of your own.

Make sure a guy always washes his hands and nails thoroughly after he's touched your anus or rectum before he puts his fingers anywhere near your vagina.

Oral Sex

NTK. The technical terms for this type of sex are *fellatio* when it's performed on a guy, *cunnilingus* when performed on a girl. But you probably know it better as going down on someone. It involves putting your lips, tongue, or mouth on the other person's genitals (though we hope for the sake of your partner you won't invite your chompers to the party!). It can be done to each other at the same time. That's known as 69, something that requires a good deal of coordination and concentration.

One good thing about our oral-aware culture is that more women seem to be insisting on a little sumpin' sumpin' as well.

So if one partner goes down on the other, it's reasonable to expect, or at least request, the other partner do the same in kind.

Risk factor. It's not as safe as you think. True, getting pregnant isn't a possibility (sperm cannot swim from your stomach to your uterus.) But contracting an STI is a very real concern. He can give it to you if he has a sore or lesion on his penis or if his pre-cum (preseminal fluid) or ejaculation carries an STI (something you won't know just by looking). And you can give him one if the fluids lubricating your vagina seep into a cut or tear in the skin in and around his mouth.

There's one STI in particular that can have a scary effect on your oral health. Oral HPV infection (human papillomavirus) is the strongest risk factor for throat cancer. Experts have seen a dramatic increase in the diagnosis of this disease among women in the past 30 years, almost 335 percent since the 1970s.

How to stay safe. Use a condom every time you do it. We know what you're thinking: *Who uses a condom for oral sex?* Covering up may seem like a total pain in the ass. But we have a responsibility to let you know why it's so essential, even if pregnancy isn't on the table. Some sort of barrier that keeps fluids out *must* be used to prevent HIV and other STIs when you're going down on him, and the same for when he's going in on you. Plastic (aka "Saran") wrap doesn't cut it for blow jobs—it's likely to tear. He might want to use it when he's going down on you, which is passable protection (a dental dam is the absolute best choice). But when you're doing the oral work, always use a latex condom. We mean it. It's not one of those things you know you *should* do but sometimes flake on, like flossing or sending thank-you notes. It's one of those things you can't live without, like seatbelts or health insurance. You can end up with an incurable disease like herpes or AIDS. Do you really want to risk that for a stupid five-minute blow job, which, let's be honest, is mostly about his pleasure? Of course not. That's why companies invented flavored condoms.

At the very least, please make sure you don't let your lips touch a guy's penis until you've surveyed it carefully for bumps or lesions and you've asked him point blank about the last time he was tested and what the results were. Even then, know that you're still taking a big gamble.

Analingus (AKA Rimming)

NTK. This is any sexual activity involving the mouth and/or tongue stimulating a partner's anus and inside his or her rectum. Also known as rimming, it may sound freaky, interesting, or disgusting to you, but some people find it pleasurable. There are many nerve endings around your butthole, and some people like it when they're stimulated with a sucking, probing, or licking sensation.

However, know that dining at the entrance to a poop chute is not like eating in a white-cloth establishment. While only trace amounts of feces are stored in your anus and rectum, it's important you bathe or shower regularly and well enough so that there's no chance of transferring these nasties to your partner's mouth.

Risk factor. It's moderately high for STIs. We're about to get a little gross here, but if one of you wiped too hard going to the bathroom, or you had a really big bowel movement, you may have tears in the skin. This is more of an issue with anal sex (we'll get to that in a moment) where you'll have contact with fluid that is more likely to carry STIs, but still, it's possible. Where there are tears, there may be blood, and that can get transferred very easily to the mouth, especially if it has any cuts. **How to stay safe.** Use a condom or a dental dam (a sheet of latex usually employed in dentistry) every time. And be sure that the rim-ee scrubs up good and clean before and after. We're talking soap, water, washcloth, baby wipes, wet-naps— the whole nine yards.

Vaginal Intercourse

NTK. Ah, the granddaddy of them all. It can involve penetration and thrusting, the girl moving up and down if she's on top, and a whole other mess of crazy positions we won't go into here. And, contrary to what horny guys have claimed since the dawn of time, yes, even just the tip counts.

Risk factor. Very high. Obviously, if a guy ejaculates in a vagina without a condom, she can get preggo. In fact, 85 out of 100 times the girl *will* get pregnant.

If he has any sort of STI, you are at high risk of getting it, too. What can increase transmission rates even more is if you cut yourself shaving down there, or you irritated the skin with a tampon. Remember, even pre-cum carries STIs like HIV, so even if you decide to stop doing it after the first penetration, you've still exposed yourself.

How to stay safe. Use a condom every single mother-lovin' time to reduce the risk of STIs. As for preventing pregnancy, you can use either hormonal birth control or a barrier method such as the diaphragm—a soft, rubber cup that fits over your cervix and keeps sperm out.

Anal Intercourse (or Anal Sex)

NTK. Few girls feel pleasure the first time they get poked with a penis or any other object in their rear. But if they are open-minded, can withstand the initial pain, and take their time with a boatload of lube, a lot of them find it's an enjoyable experience. Even a huge turn-on. For other experimenters, it's something they pretty much never want to repeat. And that's totally fine if you're one of them.

Guys generally like to do anal because the constriction around their penis is a little tighter than what they experience when they're penetrating the vagina. No wonder the Centers for Disease Control reports that the number of heterosexuals who are having anal sex has nearly doubled since 1992.

Depending on whom you believe, the number of people who have anal sex ranges from 24 to 56 percent. It's thought that more teens are doing it because they think it's a good way to have sex without risking pregnancy. But that's a dangerous assumption.

Risk factor. Super-duper high. It's for all the reasons we went through in rimming, but to the nth degree. Since the object that's penetrating you—the penis—is a lot larger than the tongue and the opening to your backdoor, there's an even greater risk the delicate skin will tear when a guy thrusts in and out. Also, your anus doesn't self-lubricate like your vagina does, so the friction poses even more of a risk. For this reason, it's essential to use lubrication.

He's at risk, too. If infected blood from your rectum or anus gets into the hole at the end of his penis, he'll get whatever bug you have. (Keep in mind that it's common to have bleeding or pain in your butthole after anal. The cause could be something as harmless as hemorrhoids, but sores and sore-ness could also be signs of an STI.)

About the only bright spot here is that you can't get preg-nant—technically. But that's only if what's going in your der-riere comes straight out and stays as far as possible from your V-zone. (Which is something it should do regardless. You *never* want to let anything near your vulva or inside your vagina if it's already had its fun in the chocolate playground next door.)

What if he keeps spurting ejaculate a little too enthusiasti-cally when he leaves your body? Or he pulls all the way out and misses his target? If your anus is lubricated or you're wet from arousal, there's a good chance that he might slip into hole number one accidentally. All of these possibilities make it so crucial to have *protected* anal sex every time.

How to stay safe. Always, always, *always* make the guy wear a condom. And since the anus is not naturally lubricated, it's important to use lots of water-based lube. Don't ever use oil-based lotions or creams, since they can cause latex to tear (carefully read the labels to make sure your lube is oil-free).

If you do anal, you need to get tested regularly just as if you were having vaginal sex. But you also have to tell your doctor that you're having this type of sex because the regular tests won't detect STIs in your rear. It may be embarrassing to speak up, but it's nowhere near as painful as getting a disease.

On the subject of talking, make sure you're okay with telling your partner the moment anal feels uncomfortable to you or if you change your mind at any point in the act.

Reconsidering the Rules of Sex?
What to Do

Any time you're thinking about sex, look at it as an issue of *comfort*; that is to say, your level of ease with each activity. Whether your guy thinks an activity is "real sex" or not is irrelevant.

Of course, you have every right to carry both your V-card and your head high. Or to proudly let your freak flag fly for all the world to see. But membership in either camp—or any point on the sexual spectrum in between—doesn't give you the privilege of "hating on" other people. Saying stuff like "Good girls don't give it up" or "She hasn't had sex yet? What a loser" is harmful to everyone and it's gotta stop. Instead, save your brainpower to contemplate your *own* experience. Ask yourself the following things:

- What level of activities do you believe you're truly ready for?
- How intimate does each sexual activity feel to you, regardless of whether people say it's "real" sex or not?
- Is what you're doing as safe as possible?
- Are you doing it with the right person?

Whenever you think it's right to take the step from virginity to more experienced territory, choose wisely. Do it with someone who is "good" because they're kind, decent, and respectful.

And when you experiment with each stage of sex, don't fool yourself into thinking one type is safe and another is not. The only way to prevent pregnancy and STIs 100 percent is to abstain from sex altogether. If there's any possibility of exposure to genitals or bodily fluids, you absolutely must use protection. (We'd tattoo this on your forehead if we could, but there are probably laws against that.) Please remember this any time someone tries to tell you that a certain type of sex isn't a biggie. It *is*!

👍 What to **SAY** to His **LIES**:

✓ "Yeah, actually it is sex. Look it up!"

✓ "It counts as sex for me, and that's not something I want to do just yet."

✓ "If there's a chance I can get pregnant or an STI, it's just as serious as intercourse."

✓ "Whatever you call it, you can still get an STI and I can get pregnant. That's not something I take lightly."

✓ "Anything that involves body fluids or touching privates is still really risky and it makes me uncomfortable."

✓ "Even the tip of your penis is still your penis. If it's in my vagina, that's still sex."

✓ "Being safe and healthy is more important to me than being a virgin. And this thing you want me to do isn't that safe."

👉 What to **DO** if You Already Bought the **LIE**:

If you've done something sexual and don't want to do it again, say so. Be emphatic! Make it crystal clear, and know that you have every right to "go back" on your actions or change your mind, even if you've already had every type of sexual activity together. What matters is if you're ready for it **now**, not any other time in the past or future.

Q&A

Q: I was fooling around with a guy, and his penis went in me a little bit, but then he took it out. He didn't come and I didn't either. So, did I really have sex?

A: Unfortunately, yes. But the unfortunate part is that it sounds as if you didn't use protection. Even if neither of you climaxed, there's still an outside chance that one of his swimmers made it inside you.

Your next step, after getting tested for pregnancy and STIs, is to figure out how you feel about this. If you're not as much of a virgin as you thought you were, don't beat yourself up about it. Call it virgin-ish or virgin-esque—it's really up to you to define the experience. And it's important that you make sex a positive thing going forward. So don't do it again if you don't feel ready. And if you do want to try again soon, make sure you use protection every time.

Q: My guy hasn't had sex yet but likes to have my fingers in his butt. Does that mean he's gay?

A: Just as there's an incorrect assumption that all homosexual guys love anal, there's an equally large misconception that if a guy likes it when a finger or any other item is inserted in his butt, that he must be gay. So not true. As long as the object going in his anus is not a penis or something held by a dude or strapped to a man, then the guy is straight. Case closed.

LIE #2

"Guys are built to cheat."

MYTHS ABOUT MONOGAMY, INFIDELITY, AND WHO—SURPRISE!— IS NAUGHTIER BY NATURE

🐕 Other Ways He **MIGHT** Say It

✗ "Men are not supposed to be monogamous, but women are."

✗ "Men are ruled by their sex drives."

✗ "Dudes have urges they can't control."

✗ "Boys will be boys—you just have to accept they'll cheat."

👉 The **TRUTH**:

We love the logic behind this one. It assumes that men have all the self-restraint of an unleashed puppy at a squirrel park.

Though they may not want to be treated like animals, when guys use the "I don't control it, it controls me" excuse to write off their bad behavior, they're the ones putting themselves in the doghouse.

The Strongest Survive

The idea that a guy needs to bang everything that moves before he gets to his grave is found in evolutionary theory. Here's the gist of it: Men want to make sure their genetic code gets passed down to as many offspring as possible. To do this, they need to have sex—lots of it and preferably with as many women as possible to increase the chances of their sperm surviving.

While all this was true thousands of years ago, we've had some significant upgrades in the software for Man 2.0 since then. With advances in DNA testing and fertility treatments, he can make absolutely sure that it's his sperm that survives in a partner. And if you ask women, they conclude that humans can do some pretty amazing things beyond knocking boots. Nevertheless, guys argue that they still operate on outdated hardware that hasn't caught up with all the amazing things people do outside the physical.

Changing the Definition of Cheating

When you try to define cheating, you first have to acknowledge that it's intertwined with what it means to be in a relationship. And that means something different to just about everyone who's in one.

Back in the Neanderthal days women really did have to pop out as many kids as possible before they dropped dead—by age

30. Even a couple of centuries ago, being with one partner for life wasn't that long, since the human expiration date was in one's 40s. Now, of course, we can keep kicking well past 100. If you get hitched at 21, that's a loooong time to stay chained to your old man. As a result, people marry later and many couples end up divorcing, some multiple times. It's not only likely that few parents are still together; many of those who are may not even like each other very much. With a new celeb or politician called out for infidelity every week, how many people can even name one relationship role model?

Who Really Cheats and Why?

Cheating rates among the general population vary, depending on where you get your statistics: as low as 22 percent for guys and 14 percent for women, and as high as 70 percent for dudes and 55 percent for chicks. However, when it comes to straying, guys are more likely to justify it, even blame the partner, saying they weren't getting enough sex at home. But guess what ladies? They

The Real Deal with Sex Addiction

SEX ADDICTION IS CHARACTERIZED by symptoms such as having many affairs, jeopardizing your health by having risky sex, and possessing the inability to connect in healthy relationships. Some people question whether this diagnosis is really just a convenient way of justifying bad behavior. But the line between a regular 'ole cheater and someone who is a sex addict is that you can't fall back on saying you have an addiction and need rehabilitation only when you get found out!

aren't the only ones straying. Figures from a national survey of American behavior show that 15 percent of women under 35 have cheated on a spouse, a stat that's 3 percent higher than it was in 1991. Who knows? Experts surmise that women may step out on their guys at a rate three to four times higher than they admit.

Cheating: What to Do

So don't let the "but we're hardwired for it" excuse fool you. At the same time, check yourself on manipulating or threatening him to get him to say he'll commit when he doesn't really want to. You're setting yourself up for heartache.

Have specific perimeters and clear expectations. While dating and crushes are part of growing up, steering clear of unnecessary drama, STIs, and unintended pregnancy is paramount.

👍 What to **SAY** to His **LIES**:

✓ "Possession of a penis doesn't automatically require you go sticking it in everything with a heartbeat."

✓ "Just because you think guys are hornier doesn't mean you don't make decisions. Let's figure out the rules and both commit to living by them."

✓ "If we are having an exclusive relationship we need to say it, if we aren't we need to say that, too. Neither of us needs the drama or the STIs."

✓ "Being a real man means honoring commitments. You need to be honest with me about what we are doing."

✓ "If we can't agree on our relationships rules, it's not up to me to compromise."

☞ What to **DO** if You Already Bought the **LIE:**

Don't ever think you have to do certain things to make sure your guy doesn't cheat, like having more sex than you want or engaging in a certain kind that doesn't feel good to you.

What matters more is what you expect from him. Any guy who tells you that you're nuts for wanting a committed partner is a poor excuse for a man. If he breaks his commitment, you have no obligation whatsoever to put up with it.

Should he cheat, you need to make a choice whether you want to stand by him or not. A few things to keep in mind: Guys make mistakes early on in relationships, especially when they're young. And sometimes if the ground rules aren't clear, he may assume certain things were okay with you that aren't. The fact that he cheated doesn't automatically make him a bad person, but you are both young. Though this is a formative time in dealing with loyalty and trust, you also don't have to deal with adult financial considerations, in-laws, custody of children, and crazy Jerry Springer-types. Remember that you may live to be 101, and that is a long, long way away.

Can This Relationship be Saved?

WE CAN'T PREDICT what will happen to your relationship if one of you screws up, but studies of married couples may give a clue or two. In instances where one partner had an affair, 34 percent of couples ended up getting divorced, 15 percent stuck it out and ended up having a healthy marriage, and a little over 50 percent stayed hitched but called their union unhappy.

Q&A

Q: Are there any big tip-offs that can tell you if a guy is going to cheat?

A: Statistically, your guy may be prone to cheating if you've been together a long time, he's had a lot of sex partners in the past, you live in a city, and he thinks about sex many times a day. Beyond that, there are personality characteristics like selfishness (does he always help himself first), narcissism (wanting to be wanted by other people to the point he gets off on being desired), and chauvinism (he grew up in a culture where women were supposed to be subservient). The other big factor is options. If he's a rock star who has groupies begging for his autograph, you can't blame him for doing a double take with a few. Studies show that availability of willing partners increases a guy's vulnerability to cheat, especially when coupled with a basic insecurity about whether he's really into the relationship.

Q: My guy told me he slept around behind his girl-friend's back. If he cheated on her, will he cheat on me?

A: Probably. But don't panic quite yet. You need a little more information first. How did it happen and how frequent was the cheating? You also need to ask how he dealt with it and what he learned. If his biggest take-away was, "Next time I'll get a separate cell phone to text from so I don't get busted," chances are he'll be up to no good eventually. But if the experience made him prioritize changing his bad behavior, he may try harder to control it in the future. You just have to be sure he's being straight with you.

Q: Can you "cheat-proof" a relationship?

A: Do you have a jail cell in the back of your closet? Because putting a guy behind bars is pretty much the only way you can control him at all times. Do you want to be a girlfriend or a parole officer? Learn to trust your gut and pick guys who are clear about their intentions and stick by their word.

Q: My guy won't let me near any of his gadgets. If I'm within two feet of his cell phone or computer he gets really agitated. What could he be hiding?

A: Something bad. We suggest you don't stick around to find out what—or who—it is. We aren't saying you need to exchange passwords and have a joint account, but he is acting in a suspicious manner.

Q: My boyfriend had oral sex with another girl, but says that since he didn't have sex with her, it wasn't cheating. It ended up being a huge fight where I ended up being blamed for being crazy. I think it is cheating. Who's right?

A: Well, one thing is for sure: His treatment of you is definitely not right. This is why it's so important to spell out from day one what is and is not okay in terms of intimacy with someone else. For some people, a kiss can be way more intense than intercourse. Since he can't be straight with you about exactly what he did or what it meant, you could conclude that he actually did have sex with her and lied about it. Cheaters will always take the path of least resistance, and "hooked up but didn't have sex" could be all it takes to clear his conscience. Here's what you need to do: Get tested for any STIs he might have passed on to you. Then go tell your boyfriend you have a new definition of sex: It's with anyone else but him. Because his ass is dumped, effective immediately.

LIE #3

"You're a slut if you've had sex with a lot of guys."

WHY BOYS GET RESPECT FOR SLEEPING AROUND AND GIRLS GET A BAD REPUTATION

🐈 Other Ways He **MIGHT** Say It

✗ "Tell me how many guys you've slept with—I won't judge you."

✗ "You should be open about your sex life, everybody is."

✗ "Girls who have a lot of sex are sluts, but guys who do it are studs."

✗ "Nice girls don't sleep around."

☞ The **TRUTH**:

A girl who takes charge of her sex life by sleeping with whomever she wants, whenever she wants, may not have as much power as she thinks. It is still something people can hold against you, no matter how open-minded they seem to be.

Playing Fast and Loose

Maybe you get the idea that you are supposed to embrace your sexuality through casual hookups, then broadcast all the intimate details on your blog. It's even a path to fame. Reality shows are a test of who can outskank, outfight, and outdrink the others to get on the next season of *Rock of Love*. As long as you "own it," anything goes.

A lot of teen girls seem to be living down to that behavior, too. One elite New Jersey high school made national news in 2009 when a "slut list" was discovered. For ten years, students at Millburn High School ranked the hottest girls who were perceived to be sexually experienced. In this case, being promiscuous can be a marker of status as well as a form of so-called bonding with other girls.

Why It Could Be Good to Get Around

Having sex like a man traditionally has—that is, in bulk quantities—can help some women perfect their skills in bed and figure out what they want from a long-term partner. Still, studies show that most women don't have the same outlook on bed-hopping as men. When asked about their feelings on casual sex, 80 percent of guys said it was a positive thing, but only 54 percent of women did. The guys were also more likely to say they were sexually satisfied, confident, and content after an experience than women.

What's in a Number?

How much people actually get around may surprise you. Guys ages 30-44 report having had six to eight sexual partners in a lifetime, while women ages 30-44 say they've had an average of four partners total. But these average numbers are deceiving. Women are more likely to shave off a few partners from their total in studies for fear of being judged. And the averages could be skewed by high and low extremes. About 20 percent of men and 31 percent of women in the U.S. have had only one sex partner.

Players and Flag Planters

EVER WONDERED WHY girls get called "sluts" but there isn't a derogatory term for a guy who sleeps around? It's a frustrating double standard. The closest terms would be *himbo* or *man-whore*, but remember, both are takeoffs of female words, and they imply that the other or opposite version is negative.

Whatever your number is, it's not necessarily a good idea to broadcast it, and especially not it in a text or via webcams. Of course you shouldn't be ashamed about your experience. But in intimate relationships, it can be used against you. A guy may ask about the number of boys you've been with, telling you that if you really love someone, you should know everything about their history.

Smart Casual?

SOME FASCINATING FACTS about sex without strings:

- Guys are more likely to want a friend to find out that they had casual sex. While women don't blab about it as much, unlike guys they tend to have higher standards of attractiveness for a casual sex partner.
- Eighty-five percent of women wouldn't consider having sex with a man unless they kissed first; only 46 percent of men said the same thing.

This conversation is always a win/lose proposition, and the girl is almost always a loser. That's because guys may say that they want a girl with experience, but when it comes down to it, many of them freak when they start imagining the faces from your past and the penises attached to them.

And just as a guy may wonder about your character if you don't reply with what he thinks is the perfect number for a nice girl, you may judge him if he hasn't had enough or has had too much sex. Unless you bring a polygraph machine to bed, there's no good way to tell if either one of you is lying anyway.

The Real Risks of Sleeping Around

Even if you don't care what people think about your sex life, you do need to care that there are consequences beyond your reputation.

Every time you sleep with someone, there's a new risk of exposure to an STI. You can take all possible precautions, but nothing is 100 percent effective. So people who have multiple partners and do everything "right" are still more likely to have an STI. It's like a raffle: the more tickets you buy, the more likely you are to win. And this is definitely one prize you do not want to win.

Also, if you get pregnant, it's possible you won't know who the father is. If that seems like a crazy scenario that's only fodder for the trashy episodes of Maury Povich, it happens way more frequently than you know. Think it sucks to talk about how many people you sleep with? Imagine how bad it might feel to admit to a bunch of guys who saw you as only a one-nighter that they need to take a paternity test.

Guys have loose lips too, and especially when e-mails, texts, and other digital communications are permanent, what they say about you can be out there for a long, long time. It doesn't even matter if they don't understand that you're not doing it because you're damaged or depressed, or that you're actually *choosing* to have sex with whomever you want. If you decide at some point you want something more committed from a guy, he may have to come to terms with the fact that you weren't quite so selective in the past.

Why should you care about this? Because some boys think that if someone is easily "taken" by a lot of guys, that they're not really worth having long-term. This is a terribly hurtful assumption, but still, a lot of guys believe it. And studies show that you're more likely to be rated as attractive to guys if you seem discriminating.

We hope that whomever you end up with for the long haul will not judge you on your past but value what your experience brings to the present. Still, you need to know the reasoning behind dumb expressions like "why buy the cow when you can get the milk for free?" Clichés shouldn't rule your life, but sometimes it helps to have a good comeback prepared for when you hear them.

Mean Girls and Sex

Slut shaming is not just a locker-room phenomenon. Research shows that when teen girls feel threatened by one another, they'll get revenge by labeling the sex lives of others in a negative way, true or not. Surely you've seen how girls try to elevate themselves, often to get a guy's attention, by pulling another peer out of the social hierarchy like a bad game of Jenga. A girl's sexual reputation can be the balance block that knocks everything out of whack and sends her social life crashing down around her.

Why do mean girls do it? You probably saw it first in middle school when a girl got a rep for being sexually advanced just because the development of her body was outpacing everyone else's. You're actually more likely to become a target if guys find you attractive.

Or maybe a girl did some things sexually that others wouldn't at an early age but then stopped. She could have been the make-out queen in sixth grade then a virgin until marriage, but the semi-slutty reputation lives on. (Sadly, being teased, ostracized, or demeaned by another girl tends to make young women have sex at earlier ages and have more partners.)

Recently, harassment has been taken to a whole new level: One survey found that almost 27 percent of girls ages 12 to 17 were involved in serious fights or attacks on other girls in the past year. Harassment also plays out in digital abuse, which includes passing along a rumor via text, e-mail, voice mail, or posts on social networking pages.

Words to Love By

"Men who think that a woman's past love affairs lessen her love for them are usually stupid and weak."
—Marilyn Monroe

Enjoying Your Sexuality: What to Do

Embracing your body and discovering all the pleasure it can give you is part of being alive. You don't have to dial down your sexuality for guys or wait for them to notice you.

But just because you're allowed to hook up with anyone you want simply doesn't mean you have to do it with everyone because you can. Even more critical is learning how to choose respectful partners who will appreciate, not judge you, based on your experience.

The only person who reserves the right to comment on your sex life is you. And you can choose to broadcast it or take the fifth. If you're asked about your "number" by a guy, you can joke with him to break the tension or just plainly state that it's none of his business. Don't let him bait you into revealing something with excuses like "I told you mine, now you have to tell me yours." That's a sign you won't live up to his expectations no matter what number you give him.

If you have sexual interactions with multiple partners, always use protection and get tested regularly for STIs, many of which have no symptoms. And regardless of your own activity, never critique others' sex lives.

👍 What to **SAY** to His **LIES**:

✓ "Labels are for cans, not people."

✓ "I know you're trying to make me feel bad about myself but it's not going to work. I have nothing to be ashamed about."

✓ "Some things are better left unsaid. My 'number' and yours are two of them."

✓ "Whether I've had sex 10 million times or never, it says nothing about who I am as a person."

✓ "I'm proud of who I am. Just because you're not happy with your sex life, you're not allowed to criticize mine."

✓ "It's my sex life and I get to decide what to do with it."

☞ What to **SAY** if You've Bought the **LIE**:

Do not equate your worth as a human being with your sexual history. Sexuality is a part of your personality, but not everything. If you know your worth comes from more than sex, eventually other people will, too.

If you experience negativity or harassment from other people regarding your reputation, you don't have to accept it. It is your right to feel safe and comfortable in school and at work. If a guy or girl is making you feel bad about your sexual choices, they need to check their shit at the door. Tell them to stop or report their behavior to a teacher, counselor, or supervisor. If it doesn't end, you can decide whether you want to report the harassment to the police and take legal action.

Q&A

Q: I messed around with some guys when I got to high school and had some bad experiences that made me want to stop having sex. The guys spread rumors about me, some that weren't even true, and now my reputation is trashed. I'm miserable at school but don't want to give into them by transferring. How do I change the situation?

A: You may think you're giving them power over you by leaving school or even moving to a new town, but you're not. You need to do whatever you can to take back control of your happiness. Your daily comfort is top priority, so if that means switching schools or staying put, do whatever is necessary.

Telling your parents about what's going on is scary yet important. It may mean revealing what you've done or discussing embarrassing rumors about stuff you didn't do, but they may be able to help you figure out a solution for stopping the harassment.

If it's any consolation, your reputation at this school won't matter in the long run. You'll go on to do great things beyond this fishbowl. The only reason your tormentors care now is because they're interested in you and have nothing better to do with their time. You, on the other hand, if you can't leave, or decide to stay and sweat it out, are building character in the face of their persecution. If you pair that with the talents you already possess, you'll find that it will make you irresistible to the friends and guys yet to come in your life.

Q: I don't want this guy I just met to think I'm a skank, but I really want to have sex with him. How soon is too soon to give it up?

A: There's no good answer to this question. Ideally, he's one of those smart guys who reserves his judgment of girls until he gets to know them, and he won't bail just because of what does or doesn't happen on the first date.

We'll say this: If you want a relationship with the guy, putting it off as long as you can is usually helpful. If you get to know a guy's conscience before you're up close and personal with his washboard stomach, the physical part might even be more satisfying when you get around to it because you'll dig his personality, too.

And some guys assume that if you do it right away with them, you do it with everyone. Most men picture the girl they want to be with long-term as more discerning. And if you end up wanting something more from him but it doesn't work out, you might wonder if doing it too soon played a part. Dating is hard enough as is. Why put yourself through that extra layer of stress and regret if you don't have to?

Q: How much sex is too much?

A: Is this a trick question? As long as you enjoy it, stay safe, and avoid partners you know are bad for you (best friend's BF, your teachers, most professional athletes).

LIE #4

"You can hook up with a friend without having feelings involved."

FROM BFFS TO FWBS AND ALL THE HAZY STAGES IN BETWEEN

🐕 Other Ways He **MIGHT** Say It

✗ "You can have sex like a man."

✗ "Hookups with friends don't count."

✗ "It's just sex—you can handle it."

✗ "We can have a casual thing without having feelings involved."

✗ "Lots of people who are friends have sex—it's natural."

✗ "You don't have to get so attached to every person you have sex with."

✗ "We're just friends fooling around. Why mess up a good thing by putting a label on it?"

☞ The **TRUTH**:

In theory, you shouldn't hook up with anyone you're not
friends with. You care about each other, you know their track
record, and you can experiment without getting hurt. At least
that's the idea.

Of course, the road to hook-up hell is paved with good intentions. We've heard the story a gazillion times: the girl who
thought she could handle a situation with a guy friend if they
slapped the "friends with benefits" (FWB) label on it, only to
end up falling for him and getting hurt.

That's the problem with using hazy terms like "hooking up"
to describe how girls relate to guys today. It's changeable and
unclear—being anything from kissing to sex. If you're not a
sex-hungry guys' girl, you get tagged as frigid and unevolved.
Guys will tell you "You shouldn't get so emotional about sex."
Dude, it is emotional for women. Our ability to hone in on feelings
beyond the physical is what makes girls different from guys.

The How and Why of Our Hook-Up Culture

Today, it seems as if disposable dating is the norm from middle
school until marriage. More high school seniors report never dating than those who actually go on dates, and by the time you get
to college, 60 percent of college kids have had at least one FWB
relationship. The average length of time people knew each other
beforehand was 14 months, with most situations lasting about six
months. Studies show that most hookups start out with no expec-
tation of a commitment on either side. Usually they are with a person in your social circle, someone you've known for years, or an

acquaintance you see out at the same parties. It could also be an ex who comes around again when you're both single, though you're not really friends when either of you is dating someone else.

It could also be a relationship with someone you meet randomly and who doesn't know your friends but whom you see every once in a while. You don't even have to like or respect him.

Why More People Are Doing It

We've seen the chicks on *Sex and the City* prove that you can have random sex without shame and that not every encounter has to be deep and meaningful. Sometimes hot sex is just that. What viewers forget is that, apart from the fact it is fiction, these are women in their 30s, with plenty of notches in their Marc Jacobs belts. They aren't under the same emotional and hormonal pressures that you are.

In your first relationships, there's a pretty big learning curve that often comes with heartbreak. Real people are scary up close, and you might risk being hurt. So maybe you find yourself looking for no-emotions, no-problems arrangements. That's nice initially because it gives the opportunity to explore sexuality without getting hurt in a real romantic sense. But it robs you of the ability to get to try sex with someone on a deeper, more intimate level. It might even leave you feeling embarrassed about wanting an emotional connection.

Your Brain on a Booty Call

Like it or not, there are fundamental differences when things get sexual. Your pulse quickens a little when his number shows up on your cell, you try to play it cool out with friends, stealing glances and hoping he's into you in a casual way but not wanting to appear *that* into him. Soon, this guy who you once felt totally relaxed to be around, even on greasy-hair sweats-clad days, all of a sudden makes a very different impact on your social radar.

When you get close to a guy, you get a big chemical boost of happy hormones and neurotransmitters. You then pursue them by upping the frequency of hookups or excuses for a situation to turn into one. Before long, you're inventing reasons to hang around him—"Hey, I was thinking of buying a mountain bike and I know you're the expert. Want to come over and help me look at some online?"—or putting your sexiest foot forward in public when he's around like you never did in the past. All of this in hopes that he'll notice how hot you look and want to start the happy hormonal roller coaster all over again.

It would be awesome if guys went through the same process. Usually they don't. Fiery postsex feelings of attachment might be strong for you, but they're more like a low-grade fever for him—it's just not as tender an experience on his end. He'll think it's equally casual for you because you act "so cool with everything." Little does he know you may be ready to drop a bomb that will destroy the balance of power in your friendship, possibly forever.

Turning Him from FWB to BF

Before long you may be anxious to have the "So . . . what are we doing anyway" define-this-relationship conversation, in hopes of upgrading your hook-up status to something more. Can you really pull it off? It's hard to say. One study showed that fewer than 10 percent of friends with benefits relationships progressed into dating. A lot of that could be timing-related.

The more troubling stat is that in half the arrangements, couples ended their friendships altogether. Most relationships imploded when one person confessed the slightest interest in having something beyond booty. This might be flattering for the other person because it makes them feel as if they have the upper hand. Or it could be a source of betrayal for the half-hearted one—"How dare they change the rules halfway through the game!"—and rejection for the openhearted partner.

Could Keeping It Casual Hurt You?

The jury is out on this one, mostly because there isn't much reliable research that looks at the way kids hook up today. One study of young adults found that those whose last sexual encounter was casual (about one-fifth of them) had the same emotional status as those who were in committed relationships.

But we do know that women usually report that their best sexual experiences require an emotional connection with the person. Why would we want it to be any other way? So if it doesn't go anywhere beyond sex, you still may have intense unresolved feelings that turn into hurt. The younger you are, the worse you may feel. One study showed that following an uncommitted relationship that included sex, girls under 15 were more vulnerable to depression than they were in relationships where no booty was involved.

Let's not forget that it's still sex. And that has its risks. What would happen if you got pregnant? In a relationship a guy may feel obligated to man up and take responsibility for his part in the situation. That's not the case when it's casual. And don't think that just because you're buds that he doesn't have an STI or that he'd even tell you if he did. Finding out he passed one to you can feel like a massive betrayal, sometimes even worse than if it happened with a boyfriend.

There's also your social group to think about. All may be fair in love and war, but there are no Geneva Conventions that rule friendship. If things end in a blowout, your mutual friends may be forced to take sides.

Finally, "friendly" hookups might be at odds with your long-term goal to have a real relationship one day. Treating casual relationships like a dress rehearsal for the real thing can be tricky, because what you put into a committed partnership is totally different.

Hookups: What to Do

If you think you'll be good at separating your heart from hookups, tread carefully. This is a skill you'll have to develop. Not everyone has it, and a lot depends on your personality and whether the friend in question values you enough to be honest. This is something you may only discover through trial and error.

Before you get involved, say at a party or when you're hanging out at his place and he makes a move, ask yourself these questions:

- If we hook up and he never got in touch with me again would I honestly, truly be totally fine with it?
- Can I trust him not to spill intimate details of our hookup to mutual friends?
- What will happen to our circle of friends if it goes bad?
- If this arrangement doesn't work out, will I be able to handle my emotions if he ignores me in public or flaunts a new girlfriend or hookup?
- Can I desensitize my heart? Do I really want to?

If you go through with it, follow these booty-call basics:

- Always use protection. The last thing you want is to tell the guy who can't even pencil you in for a weekend date that he needs to be at the free clinic next Friday for testing. Or that he should clear his schedule for the next 18 years because you've got his baby on board.
- Discuss your expectations upfront. Unless you two spell out the terms of your arrangement, it will be totally up to interpretation. And even if he hints that something more might happen down the road, assume that it will *not* turn into a relationship. (Yes, some guys do want more and even get hurt by girls in FWBs, but it's rare.) Don't promise more detachment than you can give.
- Have a nonjudgmental friend that you can be totally honest with on call. She can give tough love feedback if she thinks you're being used.
- When all else fails, follow the golden rule: Do unto others as you'd have them do unto you. If you get offended when he drunk texts you Friday night, don't think you can get away with it at 2:00 AM on Saturday night when the party is winding down and your only other friend around is Jack Daniels.

What to **SAY** to His **LIES**:

✓ "Let's call this what it really is, more than just friends. We need to be honest about what we both want from this."

✓ "Sex feels better for me when I'm in a relationship. I understand if you're not up for that, but you need to understand why I won't settle for anything less."

✓ "Why does this have to involve complicated feelings and
stuff? Because sex is messy. Get used to it."

☞ What to **DO** if You Already Bought the **LIE**:

If you can't call him your boyfriend but you want him to be
it, what are you still doing hooking up? Tell him in a very matter of fact way: "It's been a great [insert number of months]
together and I've had the best time with you. But I want a relationship that's going to lead to something more, and I don't
want to hold you up from getting that, too. You're an awesome
guy, but I'll probably need some time and space before we can
get back to being friends."

We recommend you go on a hook-up hiatus and get good at
dating next. Adopt a no pay, no play policy—which, by the way,
has nothing to do with expensive meals and gifts. It just means
letting a guy know he can't call at 8:00 PM to make plans for
that night and expect you to be available. (P.S. The brokest of
guys can fork out $10 for a pizza and bottle of sparkling cider
for a park date.) And remember, there are other things that
raise oxytocin levels—having a great meal, swimming in warm
water, taking a walk, getting a back massage—that don't put
you at risk of losing your heart or a buddy. At least if you're
not wrecking things by sleeping with your friends, you'll keep
more of them around to hang out with.

Q&A

Q: My FWB and I only hook up when we're drunk so it's usually on weekends. How do I deal with it the day after?

A: People often use alcohol as an excuse to make it seem like something didn't mean anything. If you're blacking out, you need to cut down on your drinking in general. And as far as this guy goes, if you can't have a hookup with him sober, maybe it's not worth it at all.

Q: Can you stay friends with an ex and hook up occasionally?

A: That depends. Do you sleep with all of your friends, male and female, new and old? We doubt it. Redefine what kind of relationship it really is. You actually have only two options: someone convenient to do when you both have no better prospects or someone you should keep in your past.

Q: Why do celebs lie and say people are just friends when they end up coming out and saying they're dating later?

A: Because they don't want people all up in their business. Thankfully, you don't have paparazzi trailing your butt to Starbucks. You can be more honest about who you're after if you want.

LIE #5

"If you can't have an orgasm with me, there's something wrong with you."

UNDERSTANDING FEMALE AROUSAL AND WHAT HAPPENS WHEN GIRLS GET IT ON

 Other Ways He **MIGHT** Say It

✗ "You shouldn't need anything more than my penis to get off."

✗ "You should be able to do it like a porn star."

✗ "Girls want to have crazy rough sex."

✗ "You're a freak if you like kinky stuff or watch porn."

✗ "You need too much foreplay before sex."

✗ "You must not like me or you'd be wetter."

✗ "You get too wet."

✗ "You should be able to ejaculate."

✗ "We have to come together."

✗ "Every girl can have multiple orgasms."

✗ "All women have G-spots, and G-spot orgasms are the best."

☞ The **TRUTH**:

Guys generally want to think of themselves as good lovers. When that doesn't happen despite their best efforts—and that's the norm for many of your first sexual encounters—they can feel a little defeated. The coolest ones will work even harder next time to figure out what turns their partner on and what can make sex a mutually thrilling experience. The bad guys use it as a good excuse to blame their partner for an inability to be blown away by his prowess.

Wait, did we say **good** excuse? Sorry, we meant ridiculous and hurtful.

People live in a world filled with crazy, unrealistic expectations of sex. Multiple orgasms that take two seconds to achieve. Earth-shattering experiences through missionary sex alone. And you're supposed to know exactly what will get your partners there without saying a word to them about it, right?

Guys may not realize it, but putting such high hopes on their penises alone is setting up their little guys for a whole mess of pressure. What they think they can pull off with girls may not just be unrealistic; in fact, it could be physically impossible outside of their porniest wet dreams.

"Giving" You an Orgasm?

Some guys place a woman's satisfaction at such a high premium that the best compliment you can give them is saying "Whoa, that was am-a-zing" after sex.

But many of them also subscribe to the idea that they bestow pleasure *on* you, like a fruit basket or the keys to a city. And that's where things get screwy. When a guy says that he can "give" you an orgasm, keep in mind the following: 1) You can "give" yourself one, too; no need to wait around for him; and 2) Maybe he can't "give" you one.

Some girls can't climax with intercourse alone, and there's nothing wrong with that. There are plenty of other ways to get pleasure. So why the obsession with penis-only peaking?

But the majority needs the help of the vagina's friendly neighbor to the north, the clitoris. It's the only part of your body that was designed specifically for pleasure. Predicting which guys will have both the skills and the stamina to keep you sack-happy, plus a similar drive for sex, however, is a whole other issue.

Does He Make You Horny, Baby?

In general, arousal in men is easier to achieve. For women, since female anatomy is more nuanced and connected to the mind, getting to the point of arousal can actually be a source of stress. Unless women have an opportunity to tune out the outside world—the statistics test coming up tomorrow, the belly jiggle, or his scratchy polyblend sheets—it can be difficult to get totally turned on.

Slippery When Wet: What's Too Much? What's Enough?

Normal lubrication is clear, odorless, and nonirritating. The degree to which your vagina lubricates isn't just connected to how hot you feel for a guy though. It's also controlled by estrogen levels and some other factors like time of the month, use of medications like hormonal birth control, your natural ph, drug and alcohol use, hormonal imbalances, and having a new partner.

Maybe you think something is "wrong" with the way you lubricate. You may be so freaked by what is happening that the so-called problem gets worse. It doesn't help matters when guys say dumb things like the following:

"You're too wet." First of all, he doesn't know how lucky he has it! There is nothing wrong with the amount of wetness down there. Most people think too much is never enough. But sometimes if a guy slips out during sex (perhaps because his penis is on the small side, and you happen to be very aroused), he may shift responsibility to your anatomy.

"You're too dry." It's no more okay for a guy to say you're too dry than it is for you to say he comes too much or too little. All women have variation in lubrication. That's why they're lucky to have synthetic lube. Using it is not "cheating." It's the way most girls unlock some of their greatest sexual experiences.

One recent study found that lubricant use during sexual activity alone or with a partner contributed to higher ratings of pleasurable and satisfying sex for women.

A guy shouldn't second-guess your need for lube—ever. It's used for very good reasons, like reducing the risk of vaginal tearing during rough or long sessions of sex, or cutting down on friction when using a condom.

As long as the lube is always water- or silicone-based, you can use as much of it as you like. Be aware that any kind that lists oil as an ingredient may break down the latex in condoms, so read labels very carefully, even if they claim they're water-safe on the packaging!

The ABCs of the Big O

A lot of guys want you to orgasm every time. Hey, so do the women! But men's expectations can turn something sexy into a lot of pressure to perform.

Masturbation

Touching yourself is hands down (pardon the pun) the best, safest, and easiest way to get off. You don't have to worry about pleasing anyone but you, or about getting pregnant, acquiring an STI, or being labeled a slut.

Just because it's not dinner-table-discussion doesn't mean most people don't do it regularly. A little less than half of girls say they've masturbated by age 19. That low number may be a case of selective memory or bashfulness: Many infants discover the pleasures of touching themselves below the belt and do it often in childhood. The self-stimulation doesn't become sexual until puberty, and it can involve fondling your breasts, thighs, clitoris, vulva, or vagina, sometimes with a toy like a dildo or vibrator in addition to your hands.

There's no right or wrong way to do it. But women are much more likely to be nearly always or always orgasmic when alone than with a partner. In a recent study, more than 40 percent of women who were living with a partner said they'd masturbated within the last month, but they have better sex. Other research shows that women who say they're dissatisfied with their body tend to start masturbating later and are less likely to receive oral sex from their partners. Funny enough, they're not less likely to perform it.

Clitoral Stimulation

This may come as a surprise: the clitoris extends far beyond what you see outside the body though you may only see the tip. Women are different in how and where they like their clitorises touched (or if they do at all). For some, rubbing too fast or hard, or right on the tip or shaft, may be uncomfortable, but for others, it's just the thing. Like near anything else in sex, the best way to find out is usually to experiment by masturbating.

Vaginal Stimulation or Intercourse

If you're one of those girls who can come through vaginal intercourse, consider yourself to be in a lucky minority. If you can't, no problem—consider yourself absolutely, positively, freaking normal.

One part of this play zone includes the most mysterious of all erogenous areas: the G-spot. The jury is out on whether women have one, and it may not exist the way most people describe it at all! Technically, it's the erectile tissue that wraps around the distal urethra and vagina. Even those who love the G-spot have mostly reported that it only enhances the orgasms they have through their clitoris, called a "blended" orgasm, and think of it as icing on the cake, not the cake itself.

Splish Splash

THERE IS A DIFFERENCE BETWEEN getting really, really wet and female ejaculation. "Squirting" or "gushing" is a highly controversial phenomenon closely associated with the G-spot. This phenomenon happens when a woman's G-spot is stimulated to the point that it fills with fluid that is ejaculated in spasms, not necessarily at the point of orgasm. Some research suggests that this fluid is like semen (male ejaculate) without sperm. However, since it comes out of the urethra and is often present in large amounts, some doctors think ejaculation is more similar to urine. About 10 to 20 percent of women experience this phenomenon, though many were embarrassed by it because they thought they were peeing.

Should You Fake It When You Make It?

The problem with guys learning how to help a girl to orgasm through trial and error is that sometimes they don't know whether or not there's been an "error" because so many women are busy faking them. He's thinking that slobbering all over your belly button gets you off because the last woman he was with made like a porn star when he jammed his tongue into her navel. Meanwhile, she was probably outlining her grocery list and moaning on autopilot while he drooled all over her stomach.

Most girls have faked an orgasm at least once. Maybe you're afraid of hurting his feelings or making him feel inadequate. Whatever you do in bed, do not go this way again. You are screwing yourself and all the women who may sleep with this guy after you by pretending to be pleased. Guide him to what you want and save the theatrics for drama class.

Think Kink!

EVERYONE'S GOT AN oddball attraction or two, and people are drawn to just about any sort of person, place, or thing you can imagine. See if you can match the terms below to the object or process of showing affection.

1. Agalmatophilia
2 Siderodromophilia
3. Oculophilia
4 Dendrophilia
5. Plushophilia

a) Liking to lick a partner's eyeball
b) Arousal from stuffed animals or having sex with a stuffed animal
c) Getting off by riding in trains
d) Arousal around statues or mannequins
e) Attraction to trees

Key: 1. d 2. c 3. a 4. e 5. b

Learning the Principles of Pleasure: What to Do

Most of what you need to know about being satisfied you learned in kindergarten. Take turns, share your toys, and treat someone the same way you'd want to be treated. Oh, and naptime together is the *best*. Especially if there are milk and cookies involved.

From your very first time with any guy, think about sex through the lens of your pleasure, not performance. Part of what makes each encounter exciting is the discovery of each person's quirks and preferences. But keep your expectations in check. You won't find any soul mate whose turn-ons mirror yours exactly. In fact, it's normal for 5–15 percent of all sexual interaction to be dissatisfying or dysfunctional. Talk through your concerns with your partner—guys want to learn about sex and how to make you happy. Don't do them the disservice of lying to them by faking or staying silent when you're not satisfied.

Through Thick and Thin

WHEN IT COMES TO PENISES, 90 percent of women prefer a wide penis to a long one, according to a new study. But men say length is more prized. Also, 85 percent of women say they are satisfied with their partner's penis size, but only 55 percent of guys are cool with their own dimensions.

When you do come, an orgasm is an orgasm. Which is to say, fan-freaking-tastic! It doesn't matter how you have it—clitoral, vagina, G-spot, or some mix of these. You shouldn't feel pressured to have "multiples" or to "squirt" if you don't or aren't interested. Don't let any guy tell you that how you come or how often is inferior. As long as you're satisfied, it's all good! And the way you lubricate is totally fine, too. Sex is sloppy and sometimes requires a little outside help to make it that way. If your guy can't deal with it, find someone else who will actually get off by appreciating your beautiful body.

And if you want to experiment with toys, fantasies, role-play, or other kinkier methods to bring your mind into the body game, no one should dissuade you from pushing sexual boundaries. Babeland.com and AdamandEve.com have a good selection of toys and both support philanthropy that deals with healthy sexuality.

👍 What to **SAY** to His **LIES**:

✓ "How would you know what turns every woman on?
Do you have a vagina?"

✓ "We're all different. The way my body reacts is perfectly
normal."

✓ "Let's focus less on you getting me off and more on us just
enjoying time together."

✓ "There are plenty of other ways to get me off than just
your penis."

✓ "Just because my body doesn't usually react one way says
nothing about your skills. Please don't take it personally."

✓ "I don't like doing that. Why not let it go and focus on stuff
we both like?"

✓ "Actually, some girls can come this way, and some can't.
Some want to and some don't. I personally . . ."

✓ "It's okay that you don't know exactly what to do. Let me
show you what I like."

✓ "I'm a real girl. If that's not enough for you, by all means
go home to your onscreen chicks."

✓ "Sure, the girls in porn are begging for more—they are
getting paid for it!"

👉 What to **DO** if You Already Bought the **LIE**:

If a guy insists that every woman he has been with has
come one certain way when he has had sex with them, feel
free to let him know no man has a 100% track record. There's
only one way for him to know what's good for you: Tell him.

You can also point out that he's fooling himself if he
assumes that the girls in porn get off from every little slap
and swirl on screen. They're actresses, they get **paid** to like
it, Einstein. Some might enjoy it, but they probably delight
in it as much sitting in traffic. It might be the craziest blow
job he's ever seen, but it's still part of the j-o-b, son. And he
should never manipulate you into to feeling that "all" girls
like anything whether it's rough or tender.

If you haven't yet come on your own or with a partner,
don't feel bad or that you should be in a rush to do so. Even
the most giving partners can't please you all the time, so take
charge of your own satisfaction. Read erotica. Play with toys.
And get to know your body in and out. Having an orgasm is
not an either/or situation. You have all sorts of options and
paths to pleasure.

Q&A

Q: I like this guy, but his penis is freaky looking. And
honestly, balls in general are pretty gross—all
wrinkly and jiggly. Is it bad that I'm not attracted to it?

A: What, the Joe the Camel meets a weird one-eyed
snake look isn't working for you? It's normal to be
intimidated by a guy's anatomy. You'll probably get used
to it in time, but for now, let him know you need to take
things slowly and don't push yourself into doing anything
that you'll need therapy to recover from later.

Q: I didn't know that I wasn't having an orgasm with my boyfriend when we had sex until I masturbated alone. Now I know what all the talk is about! Do I have to tell him that it didn't happen before?

A: Nah, but when the same tricks he uses don't get you off in the future, you can gently let him know you read something about a new technique you wanted to try and that you'd like to show him how to do it. Is it lying? A little bit. But if it spares his feelings and leads to amazing new feelings at his hands, we'll grant you a pass on this fib.

LIE #6

"If you're attracted to a girl, you're a lesbian."

EXPERIMENTATION AND YOUR SEXUAL IDENTITY

🐾 Other Ways He **MIGHT** Say It

- ✗ "Sexuality is black and white—you're either gay or straight."
- ✗ "Being gay is a choice."
- ✗ "If you like girls, you're just confused."
- ✗ "If you like girls it's only because you haven't been with a real man yet."
- ✗ "You can't have real sex if you're gay."

☞ The **TRUTH**:

Plenty of young women are taking a cue from celebrity sexual tourists like Lindsay Lohan, Angelina Jolie, and Katy Perry, kissing girls and really, **really** liking it. One study published found that same-sex experimentation among women has increased 7 percent since 1992. Whether that means that greater numbers of girls are jonesing for their own or that they just feel freer to admit it, a more tolerant attitude toward homosexuality has helped the girl-curious explore their urges in private and public.

But even if it's trendy and safe in some places, the idea of getting with a girl could cause some anxiety in one spot where it counts, your head. You might feel stressed about not knowing what you really want, or by being judged by guys or your family for a same-sex crush. Likewise, if it's something that's pushed on you by friends or a boyfriend, it can make you feel really conflicted about what to do.

You may wish sexuality were more certain, but at this step you can simply acknowledge the many nuances of gray that some girls feel for other girls at this stage in life. We'll get you started on the subject with a quick tutorial on what science knows and has yet to discover about homosexuality.

What Makes You Gay

Researchers pretty much agree that your sexual orientation has little to do with which sports you played as a kid or whether you listened to Madonna on repeat for years. It's also not about being liberal, conservative, religious, communist, pretty, ugly, or anything in between. It's about being human and born with a certain genetic makeup.

The best evidence of this comes through studies of identical twins. They have the same genetic codes, and research has shown that if one identical twin is gay, there's about a 50 percent chance the other one is too, even if they didn't grow up in the same home.

And one gene is not necessarily responsible, but rather a set of characteristics on the X chromosome, which is the one that moms pass to their kids. Homosexuality may also be influenced in the womb by hormones. If you were exposed to more testosterone (the male sex hormone) when you were just a bump on your mom, you may like both girls and guys.

Factors of Attraction

About 96 percent of Americans identify themselves as straight—depending on which studies you go by—and anywhere from 2 to 5 percent of people say they're homosexual (and you know because of the stigma, this number is grossly underestimated). Whether they declare their preference at age 6 or 66, most people know what their preferences are by their late teens.

Measuring this attraction in a lab setting is pretty tricky. A lot of studies on homosexuality involve showing people porn or explicit photos while hooked up to machines in a clinic. Still, there are some interesting differences between the sexes and how people identify their orientation. When shown photos of sexy people, straight guys tend to get turned on by those of women but those not of men. Homosexual guys are the opposite—the photos of guys get them going, while the women do nothing for them. What's different about women is that they get aroused by both male and female erotica, regardless of whether they identify as lesbians or heterosexuals.

Most experts in the scientific community think that female sexual orientation is a little like Silly Putty: It's flexible and has the ability to be imprinted with all the shades of its environment. So what does it mean when you have a "girl crush" but you're usually more into guys? And how much can it tell you about whom you'll go for tomorrow or in 10 years?

Just a Phase?
What a Same-Sex Attraction
Says about Your Sexuality

It's totally normal to wonder what it would be like to kiss a girl you're close to, but that doesn't mean that you're necessarily going to do it or that you should apply one random urge to your sexuality as a whole. A lot of preferences get sorted out in college, where being away from family and having more freedom to let loose (often with the assistance of alcohol) allows girls to be LUGs—that is, Lesbians Until Graduation. Once they're out in the working world, being with a girl doesn't mesh with their goals. It's especially true for people who grew up with a mom and a dad and want the same nuclear family experience. Of course, you can raise kids with a woman or pop out a baby with a guy and continue to have relationships with women, but it's just not as common. That's why it's a little more likely that a woman would identify as a lesbian for a time, then as a heterosexual for the remainder of her life.

You're Just Not into Them:
What if Guys Don't Do It for You

If the girls at your school primarily date guys, it can feel pretty isolating when you aren't as boy-crazy as they are. When they talk about how hot every guy is and you don't see it, you might wonder, *Is there something wrong with me?* Or if you don't get much of a charge when you hook up with a boy, you could start to worry whether you'll ever feel anything for guys at all. Does this automatically mean you're into girls? The short answer is nope. Since so many boys don't know what they're doing around a girl's ladybits at this age, you may just need to be with a more experienced guy to understand what being turned on is really about. And nervousness or not feeling confident about your body could dampen your excitement for the hook-up process in general

On the other hand, if you also have a crush so strong on a girl you shake like a phone on vibrate when you're around her, or spend so much time wondering what it would be like to touch her that you can't concentrate in class, these could be signs your attraction to girls may be more than just fleeting.

Either or Neither: Transgender Teens

If questions about attraction weren't tough enough to handle, some kids have an added challenge of feeling they aren't really the gender they were assigned to by nature or the doctor who delivered them.

The term transgender can refer to a range of different identities: anyone who feels neither one sex nor another (androgynous); someone who has physical characteristics of both sexes (e.g., hermaphroditic or intersex); or a person who feels as if he or she is actually a third gender or a perfect mix of both (bigender). Within that range, their preference for other people can go either way and also include someone who is transgender. The term transgender is not the same as transsexual, which is someone who is making the actual transition from one gender to another, with or without help of surgery, hormones, or other physical modifications.

No matter which gender you identify with, figuring out how to integrate the masculine and feminine sides is something everyone deals with. Remember, everyone has two parents, one male and one female. Meaning, everyone has some of both the masculine and feminine energy within. No person is 100 percent of one, and you're not less of a girl for liking men or women more.

There's a lot of gender blurring in our culture today, and that's good because it allows us to try on different identities as if they're boy shorts or boyfriend jeans. Just be accepting of how other people experiment in order to find theirs, whether it's temporary like guyliner or as permanent as a sexual reassignment surgery.

The Danger in Believing Gay Sex Isn't "Real" Sex

If you are bisexual or identify as a lesbian, sexual activity for you may be anything from kissing and playing with another girl's breasts to cunnilingus (AKA going down on her) and rubbing each other's vulvas together (also called tribadism). However you hook up, it's just as authentic as any other kind of sex, even if you use toys to penetrate the same way a guy might do with his penis.

That means it also comes with risks—if not for pregnancy then certainly for STIs. Giving or receiving oral sex can transmit infections like gonorrhea, syphilis, and chlamydia. And any skin-to-skin contact carries a risk of passing on HPV—that includes fingering or just grinding against each other. It doesn't matter if neither one of you has ever been with a guy; if one of your past partners has been with anyone infected with an STI, male or female, they could have passed it on. Besides, more than 80 percent of gay women have slept with a man, so it's still important to ask your partner to be tested and use protection like a dental dam or female condom during sexual activity.

Homosexuality and Your Health

If your home or community is hostile to gays, sorting out your attraction to women can take a serious toll on your body and mind. Studies show that if you're in a sexual minority, meaning gay, lesbian, bi, or transgender, in an atmosphere where straight is the norm, you're twice as likely to seek help for mental health issues or substance abuse treatment.

That's not at all to say you're sick or crazy—you just may be dealing with consequences of bullying, exclusion, or isolation your straight peers don't experience. You may not realize that you're physically exhausted from hiding your orientation or having to manage conflicting feelings. Or you may not understand how underlying sadness or anxiety could be connected to feelings of not being accepted, so you suffer in silence or minimize your troubles. Even if you're not out yet, it's a good idea to talk to a counselor or trusted adult to get a balanced perspective and find strategies to deal with any negativity that comes your way.

Exploring Your Gender Preferences: What to Do

Recognize that your sexuality right now is less about a fixed orientation and more about evolving preferences. This means that what you feel at this moment about men and women may not be fixed, either now or ever. Many girls before you have experimented with women and gone on to identify as straight, and many more will do so after you.

Whatever your conclusion, we challenge you to look at this time as a great period where you have room to try out all different identities, depending on what feels safe in your environment. It's more important for you to look for someone who you love, not a specific package you think you're supposed to want. If you end up liking something that's not the norm where you are, you might feel alone. But you're not. People who feel like you just aren't voicing it.

Remember to be conscientious about other people and where they're coming from when you explore with other girls. You might kiss one at first just to fit in or follow a trend, but there's another person on the end of those lips. Toying with people for your own titillation or attention from others is not okay. If you want to try it, make sure it's on your own terms, not to attract or turn on some guy.

The good news is that you can take your time, and keep it to yourself as long as you choose partners you trust. When you know for sure what you want—and that could be a while—it's up to you what to do with the information. Ideally, you'll be able to share it with people you love, but it's no one's business what you are. You don't have to host your own personal pride parade for being a "good" or "real" lesbian. You don't even have to use labels at all. If you do call yourself a lesbian, you can be a "dyke," "lipstick lesbian," or "chapstick lesbian," for that matter. What term you use won't lessen the intense love that you or other girls feel for each other.

Most important, being anything other than fully hetero shouldn't be a sentence to a lifetime of isolation, despair, or self-hate. There are groups listed at the end of the book to help you deal with this, but you might find that if your straight friends are cool with it, you don't have to change anything about your life.

No matter your preference, you have a responsibility be an example of a tolerant, kind approach to sexuality. Start by exposing myths and educating the ignorant with solid information, not assumptions and stereotypes. And stand up to hate in any form. Everyone needs to stop using the word "gay" to mean dumb, or slurs like "faggot" to bring someone down, and to call out those who do. Words do have meaning. People have died over them.

Finally, a word to the religious girls: It can be hard for gay women to be told their identity is against what should be moral or right. No matter your beliefs, the worst sin of all is to be a silent bystander when others are being persecuted. This passage from the Bible is inspirational, even if you're not Christian: "Speak up for those who cannot speak for themselves; ensure justice for those being crushed." And remember that people have too little time on this earth to spend it hating themselves or anyone else on account of whom they love.

👍 What to **SAY** to His **LIES**:

✓ "Why does it matter so much to you who I like? It's none of your business, really."

✓ "I'm trying to figure this out myself. Cut me some slack, please."

✓ "All you need to know about me is that I treat the people I'm into with respect and kindness."

✓ "It's sad that you have to judge me because you're not okay with yourself, but that's not going to change me, or the fact that I'm totally cool with myself."

✓ "I feel lucky that I get along with guys and girls."

✓ "I'm exploring this to make myself happy. It's not my responsibility to please anyone else."

✓ "Whoever shouts the loudest about how other people are doing something wrong is probably trying to cover up something they hate about themselves. What is it that you're trying to hide?"

👉 What to **DO** if You Already Bought the **LIE**:

If you find yourself attracted to girls, it might seem easier to just make yourself try to be straight. But you can wear the wrong shoe on the wrong foot for only so long before you stop moving forward.

Sometimes you might take a second look at women after hurtful experiences with boys, like being cheated on or abused. You may have even heard women say, "I have such bad luck it's enough to turn me into a lesbian." While you might double your wardrobe if you take that leap, don't assume a girl-girl relationship is without heartache.

Q&A

Q: I've always been attracted to girls, but I know that my parents want me to be straight. I feel like I would be letting them down if they knew how I really felt. Should I tell them?

A: For them to want you to live the life they envision is understandable, but for them to make you feel bad, either blatantly or indirectly, is inexcusable.

Start by thinking that they might feel "let down." True, it could be from religious or moral objections. But also it might be out of concern and love for you. They may perceive a harder life for you if you're openly gay, though that's not necessarily going to be true for you. Selfishly, they may want the picket fence hetero ideal they grew up with. (Of course, you can still have a loving partner and babies, just not the way they picture it.)

Find yourself a support group, either online or one that meets in your community. Make sure you hear other's experiences of coming out and have their support for when you have that talk with your family.

Remember that experimenting, being bisexual or gay adds extra stress to an already stressful time in your life. If you suspect this might be talking a toll on you, make sure you get screened for depression and have access to 'round-the-clock support, whether in person, online or on the phone. There are plenty of resources listed at the back of this book.

Q: Can you fall in love with a girl but not be sure if you're attracted to her?

A: With matters of the heart, anything is possible. Don't beat yourself up about it. Know that it could be admiration or any series of feelings that have to do with liking her style and intellect. Women morph and change with time and experience; nothing you are feeling is weird or abnormal.

Q: I borrowed my BF's laptop and found gay porn on it. It's really freaking me out because he tells me he loves me and doesn't seem gay. What's up?

A: This is a tough one because there's no foolproof way to say whether a guy is or isn't, especially when he may be still trying to figure it out as well. But we do need to tell you that if there's one sign a guy is gay, this is it. You need to talk to him about it in a safe atmosphere. He may feel judged and deny it, but don't let him explain it away ("It's my buddy's," or "It was for a project on sexuality in health class"). If he does admit feelings for a guy, it's your decision whether to stick with him as he explores them. While it doesn't feel good to be deceived by a guy who says up front that he's straight and isn't, he probably didn't mean to hurt you. Be thankful you realized this early on and have options of your own to deal with it.

LIE #7

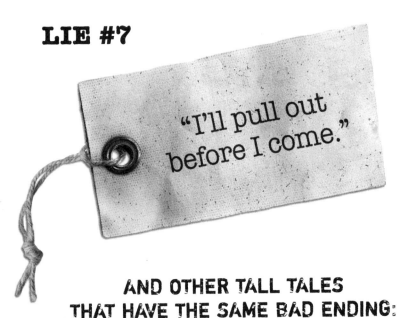

"I'll pull out before I come."

AND OTHER TALL TALES THAT HAVE THE SAME BAD ENDING: YOU BEING KNOCKED UP

🐈 Other Ways He **MIGHT** Say It

✗ "You can't get pregnant the first time you have sex with someone."

✗ "If we do it in a certain position, you can't get pregnant."

✗ "If you have sex underwater you can't get pregnant."

✗ "If we take a shower before sex, you won't get pregnant."

✗ "If you do it standing up you won't get knocked up."

✗ "We got lucky once, we'll get lucky again."

✗ "If we pray hard enough, you won't be pregnant."

✗ "We don't have sex that often, so you can't be pregnant."

✗ "I smoke and eat a lot of crap—I'm sure my guys can't swim."

✗ "If I wear tight underwear I won't get you pregnant."

✗ "If you don't have an orgasm, you can't get pregnant."

☞ The **TRUTH**:

No use pretending that sex without a condom doesn't feel good. It does, and your guy knows it.

People will tell their partners and themselves just about anything to justify a little rubber-free nookie, whether it's exaggerating their ability to pull out in time, or just some doozies about what leads to or prevents conception. Part of it could be earnest misinformation, hearsay that gets distorted like a bad game of telephone when a friend swears their cousin's boyfriend tried some sort of position or potion that worked. Even if it sounds too stupid to be believed.

Mostly, though, these lies evolved to seize a little control back from a situation where two people are out of their minds with lust and don't want to stop doing something that feels good. But there are serious problems with having unprotected intercourse and waiting until the last second for your guy to jump ship or for an old wives' tale to be effective.

Let's look at the first way a guy might try to convince you he has more control over conception than he really does when you're having unprotected sex.

The Russian Roulette of Birth Control

We're talking about the withdrawal method. That's when the man withdraws his penis from your vagina just as he feels he's about to ejaculate. He comes outside of your body, perhaps on himself, in a towel, or on another part of your body like your breasts. As he does this, he makes sure that semen doesn't spill anywhere on your vulva—that fleshy area outside your vagina. A lot of religions actually advocate this method because it doesn't involve traditional hormonal birth control or condoms, which may be against their beliefs. Hence, the "pull and pray" nickname.

Sounds like there's not much to it, right? Well, despite the seemingly simple mechanics, it's just not an effective form of birth control.

The withdrawal method has a 4 percent failure rate when practiced perfectly. Notice that last word. *Perfectly.* You may be a straight-A student with supermodel looks, a stellar personality, Serena Williams' backhand, and perfect pitch. But face it, my dear, you're not perfect. No one is. So it's pretty useless to even pay attention to a statistic like that when it's known that no one will be able to do anything perfectly 100 percent of the time.

The only failure rate stat that *really* applies to you is 27 percent. That's the percentage of times this method ends in pregnancy if it's not done correctly. Which is the way most people practice it.

What does this failure rate look like in terms of real people, exactly? Imagine 100 fantastic but just-short-of-perfect women just like yourself having sex with their partners. If they don't do it *absolutely perfectly*—like without a single, solitary drop of semen landing in their vagina or just outside it—27 of them *will* get knocked up. Guaranteed. That means you have more than a one in four chance of getting pregnant. Some freakin' terrifying odds for only a couple of minutes of fun, right? And don't misinterpret them either—it doesn't mean that if you have sex three times you'll only get pregnant on the fourth one. It means you could get pregnant the first and only time you do this.

No Laughing Matter

Q: What do you call people who practice the withdrawal method?

A: Parents.

Why It's Harder than You Think to Stop in Time

Of course, when you're all doped up on these natural love drugs, the last thing on your mind is any consequences of finishing the act, like how baby spit up would totally ruin your cute going-out tops. Or how much it would suck to bring a 10-pound human crying machine along on romantic date nights.

Your own hormonal responses aren't even the biggest biology problem you're dealing with here. As soon as he starts to have sex, physiologically his body will start deferring to the mission all healthy guys were born with: impregnate the fertile female in front of him. But he's also a red-blooded male whose body was designed to reproduce so that the species doesn't die out (even though the world is totally overpopulated now!). Even if he really cares about you and what you want, sometimes it may be just too hard to resist going all the way through with the act when his reptilian brain is cheering on his little sperminators like a manic swim coach at the state championship meet.

Houston, We Have a Problem

The withdrawal method requires that a guy be so experienced that he knows precisely when he's reaching the point of arousal where he can't stop or postpone ejaculation. That's totally up in the air every time you do it, depending on the setting, mood, and connection between the two of you. Odds are, your partner won't understand his body well enough until he's in his mid-20s to have the incredible timing and restraint that's necessary to pull this off.

Of course, it's also possible he knows he's lying when he says he'll pull out and doesn't care if that hurts you. The only thought some bad guys have when they're with a girl is how they can use her to get an orgasm. And they'll say anything to do it, especially if they're not in a relationship with her. Think about it: If all you are to him is a random chick who can get him off right this minute, what does he care if you get pregnant? It's not like *he'll* be the one who will be carrying the baby in nine months.

The reason why this method is a mess in the first place is that the responsibility is on the *guy* to make it work. It's just way too much power and trust to put in someone else's hands when lives are at stake. You need to think long and hard about how much faith you have in every sexual partner, but even more so when you're relying on a guy to pull out. You don't know what it's like on his end, what he's thinking, how his body is functioning, or even how his O-face predicts when he's about to blow. What if he pushed you down physically as he got closer? He may not mean to, but in the animalistic heat of the moment, guys can get rough. Plus, the average speed of ejaculation for guys is 28 miles per hour. Unless you wear running shoes in bed, don't bet on getting away that fast.

Another critical reason to avoid the method? It doesn't protect against sexually transmitted infections. This is what we were talking about when we said pulling out puts your life in danger, because the very real possibility of contracting HIV is reason enough to never go condomless. Not to mention all those other STIs—some incurable—that can leave you infertile and pretty darn uncomfortable.

The Top Whoppers

Urban legends about sex and pregnancy are so prevalent, it's hard to choose just the 20 that you're likely to hear. In fact, there are so many relating to your period we made a whole chapter about what you really need to know when you ride during your red tide.

For now, though, let's break down the biggies that revolve around plain old P/V sex.

1. You Can't Get Pregnant If It's Your First Time

Um, is he neglecting the laws of physics? Penis + vagina = risk of pregnancy every single time. Case closed.

In fact, the less experienced you are, the more likely you will hit the baby jackpot. Why? You may be so turned on that you're more likely to make mistakes with your birth control method or avoid contraception altogether. Approximately a quarter of teen females and 18 percent of teen males did not use a method of contraception at first intercourse. And 20 percent of teen pregnancies happen within the first months of having sex, with 50 percent taking place in the first six months.

2. My Body Is Messed Up

Unless your doctor has told you that you cannot get pregnant, you don't know this at all. But plenty of people assume it anyway: 59 percent of women and 47 percent of men suspect that they're infertile.

Unlike women, who are born with somewhere between one and two million eggs all ready to go in their ovaries, men are constantly making new sperm. This process is called spermatogenesis, and it churns out about one-half billion sperm each day of a man's life.

3. Doing It Sitting Down or Standing Up Won't Get You Pregnant (especially if you jump up and down immediately after)

Eighteen percent of young adults believe you can reduce the chances of getting pregnant by sexing while standing. But the laws of gravity are moot if a guy shoots an average 300 million sperm into your vagina when he ejaculates, regardless of the position you do it in. Even if you spend all day jumping naked on a trampoline afterward, only a few thousand swimmers may drop out of the race.

4. Douching After Sex Prevents Pregnancy

Decades ago women thought that rinsing out the vagina with a solution of water and vinegar, soda, or a store-bought formula would clear it of sperm. Now women know better: douching can actually push semen further up into their cervix and increase their chances of getting knocked up. Plus, douching in general is a bad idea. Your vagina is a self-cleaning oven; all you need are regular checkups.

5. Peeing After Sex Will Stop Sperm from Getting to Your Uterus

Not gonna do it. Urine may carry a small amount of semen away from the vaginal opening and vulva, but does nothing about the other hundreds of thousands.

That being said, it's smart for you to pee for another reasons: urinating postcoitus flushes away bacteria that could cause a urinary tract infection.

6. Using a Heating Pad Kills Sperm

While heat may slightly lower a guy's sperm count, healthy sperm are likely to survive when he ejaculates even if he's been hot tubbing. By the time the sperm are in your body, there's not too much you can do since the environment is already perfect for implanting.

7. Taking Aspirin Will Make the Sperm Unable to Fertilize an Egg

If that's all it took to prevent a pregnancy, don't you think more people would be loading up on aspirin instead of messing with hormonal contraception? The only pill that can prevent implantation after sex is emergency contraception—also known as Plan B.

8. If You Sneeze Really Hard or Do Kegels You Can Force Sperm out of Your Body

Back away from the pepper mill, babe. Sneezing may feel like a force of nature, and even if your PC muscles could crack a walnut, it's not possible. Even if you could get 299,999 million sperms out, it's baby time if there's one left in there that meets a beckoning egg.

9. You Can't Get Pregnant When You Are On Your Period

Hard to believe, but this is false! Because of the lifespan of a guy's sperm and your eggs, having sex while you are having your period doesn't mean you are safe at all.

10. You Can't Get Pregnant if You Have Sex in Water

We hate to break it to you, mermaid, but it's just not true. Aquatic sex involves a lot of risks for very little thrill and no benefits. The sperm won't "swim away," and the salt in seawater and chlorine in pool water do nothing to kill them.

In fact, even if you do it with a condom, there's an increased chance it will slip off thanks to friction due to less lubrication. There's also a higher risk you'll get a urinary tract infection when you're feeling his motion in the ocean, because there's a greater variety of bacteria there than what you're normally exposed to.

11. Wearing Fitted Underwear Can Help Him Create Less Sperm to Pass on to You

While boxers will actually help a man with sperm production, it's not clear that tighty whities will do the opposite. But keep in mind that fabric between the two of you, be it his underwear or your underwear, is just not a good barrier. So just because you keep your skivvies on, don't feel as if you are safe.

12. If You Don't Have Sex Enough You Won't Get Pregnant

One sperm, one egg: one baby. Once really is enough. Take the Boy Scout approach: Be prepared, even if you're a virgin, are having a dry spell, or are just thinking about being sexually active. Falling in love and having sex often happen at the same time—when you least expect it. And usually on the day you forgot to shave your legs.

13. A Guy with Lazy Sperm Can't Get You Pregnant

Just because a dude won't get his ass off the couch and get a job doesn't mean his sperm aren't motivated to do their duty. If they swim like Michael Phelps or doggy paddle, they'll make it to the finish line eventually if they are en route,

14. A Guy Who Has Done Too Many Drugs Will Shoot Blanks

Ah, the refrain of stoners everywhere. Drugs and alcohol have been shown to lessen the number of sperm in a man's ejaculate. And some studies suggest that smoking weed can also damage a sperm's DNA, leading to problems with the smoker's offspring. Anabolic steroids, usually taken illegally, also shrink the testicles and drastically reduce fertility.

15. A Hot Guy Can't Get You Pregnant

Have you seen Shiloh Jolie-Pitt? Proof positive it happens. The reason for this myth is that in animal studies, more attractive males tend to release fewer sperm with one partner so that they can boost their chances of having a kid with a whole range of females. Maybe your guy heard this while watching a show on wild animals, but it is too big a leap to be true in his case.

16. If You Don't Have an Orgasm You Can't Get Pregnant

Even if you don't orgasm, you can get pregnant. Even if he doesn't, his precum may contain enough sperm to do the job. How frustrating is that? The good news is that with just one little condom between you, you can both come and not think about parenthood just yet.

17. He's More Likely to Shoot Blanks if He Works Out a Lot

Most athletes have plenty of ability to impregnate women. However, some activities may have more effects on fertility than others. According to one study, men who experience grueling mountain-bicycling programs on rough terrains are apt to have lower sperm counts and more abnormalities of the scrotum than noncyclists. Jackass-aping stunts or a direct hit with a linebacker might in fact cause testicular torsion and interrupt sperm production. However, whether you are pro, amateur, or weekend warrior, this is not an excuse for not having to wear a condom.

18. It Won't Happen to People Like Us

Let's set the record straight: A sperm doesn't have a conscience. It cannot get halfway up your vaginal canal and say, "Wait a minute here . . . this tunnel looks like it belongs to a sweet kid. I'd sure hate to mess with that college scholarship she just got or crush her dreams of becoming a Broadway dancer. On second thought, I think I'm gonna hang out here instead of doing what I was specifically designed to do."

Newsflash: "Good" girls get pregnant every day. No amount of prayer or magical thinking can make a physical gate come down between a sperm and egg just in the nick of time.

19. If You Eat Certain Foods You Can't Get Pregnant

No amount of Sunny D, Mountain Dew, or any other drink will act like a spermicide, or shrink your ovaries or testicles. Same for any potions, herbs, or concoctions someone swears worked once, on someone, somewhere.

20. Pregnancy Only Happens if You Want It

Oh, reeeeally? Tell that to the 584,000 girls who end up with an unwanted, unplanned pregnancy each year. Or the women who desperately try to get pregnant but can't and resort to costly and invasive methods like in vitro fertilization. Or the cash-strapped parents of five whose condom broke.

Understanding Contraception: What to Do

Unless you want to become a mother, you need to forget everything you've heard when it comes to myths, legends, and promises you can't back up with scientific proof, including a guy's ability to pull out each and every time with perfection. If a dude puts his penis in your vagina without protection, there is a very good chance you will get pregnant. So use a condom, and/or hormonal birth control, every time you have sex.

And if you still really, really want to believe something ridiculous and quite possibly untrue, go read your horoscope.

👍 What to SAY to His LIES:

✓ "You know how babies are made, right? By people who believe dumb stuff like that."

✓ "You might be trying to ease my mind, but I know for a fact that's not true."

✓ "I didn't think you believed urban legends."

✓ "I don't know where you heard that, but you're about to hear the real truth from me."

✓ "It might feel better for you to have sex without one, but it feels scary for me. And I know you wouldn't want to make me feel uncomfortable in any way."

✓ "If you're not going to protect me from the possibility of getting pregnant, then I'm going to protect us **both** by insisting on a condom."

✓ "We'd both feel awful if you weren't able to pull out in time. Let's not risk it."

✓ "If you want to gamble, you can go do it with your money, not my body."

✓ "I'm not willing to risk getting a disease or having a baby for less than an hour's worth of fun."

✓ "Good and bad have nothing to do with it. It's about being smart enough to be safe."

✓ "I have too much going for me. I can't rely on luck to keep me from getting knocked up."

☞ What to **DO** if You Already Bought the **LIE:**

If you routinely practice unsafe sex, you are a damn fortunate girl. Thank God, the universe, your lucky stars, or whatever it is you wish on at night that you got away with it once. And then . . . Stop. Pushing. Your. Luck. For real.

If he's giving you the rubber runaround, don't be afraid to stick it to him. Make it emotional if you need to: "If you cared about me, you'd find a way to make it work." If he refuses to believe how important it is, you refuse to get anywhere near his ignorant self.

Next, you need to get tested for STIs, and do a follow-up test again in six months. Finally, monitor your body carefully for any bumps—including a big one in your stomach.

Q&A

Q: Isn't pulling out better than nothing?

A: Technically, yes. Just like the idea of running down your street in a G-string is *technically* better than having to sprint past your friends and neighbors buck naked. But neither one is an appealing or smart choice when you have the option of not doing it at all. (And yes, you *always* have that option, no matter what he says.)

Sometimes you get caught up in the moment. You're not planning to have sex. He asks just to put the tip of his penis in. You let him, thinking it won't go any further than that. Then, he puts it in a little more, pulls out, goes in a little deeper . . . deeper . . . and all of a sudden, you've progressed to full-on intercourse. So the only course of action you should take here is to tell the guy you'll enjoy the ride a lot more in a couple of hours when you have the chance to get some condoms.

Q: My guy said he pulled out with his last girlfriend and she never got pregnant, so I'm safe, right?

A: No, not at all. First, you have no idea how fertile you are compared to her. Just because they got lucky when they were, uh, getting lucky, that's no guarantee you will, too.

Also, remember what we said before: Every time a guy is with a new person, his body reacts in unpredictable ways. The mystery and novelty involved with sleeping with someone for the first time go a long way to getting a guy jacked up. So even though he may have been totally controlled with his last GF, sex with you could be a whole other thrill that's shorter than planned. Insist on condoms.

Q: If I'm on birth control does he still have to pull out?

A: Again, pulling out doesn't protect you against STIs, so you're not safe there without a condom. He could be sleeping with another girl—or guy (yeah, it happens)—on the side who may or may not be clean. Or he could have a sexually transmitted infection that neither one of you can see on the surface. He could just space out and completely forget to pull out one time that he's uberaroused when you're having sex in a new place or position that really turns him on. You may trust your partner with your body, but you need to make sure you trust him with your life as well. And he's protecting it every time he wears a condom.

And the pill is only highly effective when taken exactly as directed, usually at the same time daily. So to be doubly safe in the event you forget to pop one, go "double Dutch" by using condoms in addition to hormonal birth control.

LIE #8

"I can't wear a condom so you need to use birth control."

CONTRACEPTIVE RESPONSIBILITY AND WHAT TO DO WHEN YOU GET THE RUBBER RUNAROUND

 Other Ways He **MIGHT** Say It

---

✗ "If you take a bunch of birth control each day it will protect you from pregnancy."

✗ "I hate the way condoms feel—sex is so much better the natural way."

✗ "We didn't use a condom before and nothing happened, so we're okay."

✗ "Condoms won't keep everything out, so there's no point in using one."

✗ "If I wear two of them, it's safer."

✗ "Real men don't use condoms."

☞ The **TRUTH**:

It's hard to imagine what sex was like before hormonal
birth control (BC). Back in the 1700s and 1800s, middle-class
women got pregnant between 17 and 22 times in their life-
times! While men still only have two ways to prevent pregnancy (condoms or a vasectomy), women now have 11 ways.

More than 100 million women worldwide currently rely
on combined hormonal methods such as oral contraceptives
(a.k.a. the pill), the patch (Ortho Evra), the vaginal ring
(NuvaRing), the shot (DepoProvera), the implant (Norplant)
or IUDs (intrauterine devices). Among U.S. women who
practice contraception, the pill is the most popular choice
because it's relatively cheap, effective, and easy to get.

That doesn't mean there isn't a whole lot of confusion that
comes with all this freedom. In one recent study, when asked
to rate their knowledge of birth control pills, 78 percent of
men reported to be clueless, compared to 45 percent of
women. In addition to believing bogus info—e.g., that if you
take several pills in one day you can protect yourself even
more—there are a lot of people who buy into sexist stereotypes
attached to pill use and get dissuaded from looking into it.
Others don't really understand how newer methods work:
One study found that 20 percent of teen girls overestimate
the effectiveness of the patch and ring.

When figuring the best way to not get pregnant if you're sexually active, it pays to know about all the hormonal methods and myths out there. Even if you abstain from sex altogether, you should be aware about emergency contraception in the event a hookup goes too far. Take it from the couples who commit to holding out, but for whom "things just happen," and nine months later, a baby "just happens" to be ruling their life.

Hormonal BC:
How it Works and Who Takes It

We'll start with the most common method, the pill. There are two kinds of BC pills, those that use only the hormone called progestin, and those that use a combination of both progestin and the hormone estrogen. This is known as the combination pill, and most women who take the pill are on the combination pill.

The next most commonly used methods for women are the vaginal ring and the patch.

The ring is inserted in the vagina and releases a continuous low dose of hormones into the vagina for three weeks. At the start of the fourth week, you remove the ring and have a normal period.

The patch is a small square less than two inches big that you wear on an area of skin such as the stomach, butt, or upper arm for seven days at a time. You use a new one each week for three weeks to get a steady stream of estrogen and progestin, then go without one for the last week of the month and have a period.

Hormones like progestin and estrogen work to keep your ovaries from releasing eggs every month. If there are no eggs released, then there will be no ovum to fertilize and make a baby if sperm enters your vagina. Also, they thicken your cervical mucus, which can prevent a sperm from joining with an egg, and they thin your uterine lining, making it harder for a fertilized egg to implant there.

If you're old enough to menstruate, you can use hormonal birth control. Because you won't be ovulating, you won't have a technical menstrual period, per se, but that's what we call the "off week" when you take placebo pills or don't receive hormones because there will still be bleeding as if it were an actual period.

Combination pills come in a 28- or 21-day pack; either way, you will be taking only 21 pills that have hormones in them each month (AKA "active" pills). The remaining seven, if there are any, are just reminder pills that don't have any hormones. It is a good idea to take them anyway because you stick with the habit of taking a pill every day.

The progestin-only pills are only available in 28-day packs. You need to take one every day, specifically at the same time.

Some pills allow you to have fewer periods—as few as four per year or none at all. These come in special multi-month packs, followed by a week of low-estrogen or no-hormone pills. Some women also opt to take the 21- or 28-day pills without any breaks to cut down on the number of periods they have. Your doctor can advise you about whether this is a good option for you, and which day you should start using the pills in general.

Typically, young women use hormonal birth control to prevent pregnancy, but teens also use it for other reasons—for example, for regulating menstrual periods. Combination pills can also help prevent or protect you from the following:

• severe menstrual pain

- heavy menstrual bleeding
- menstrual migraines
- ectopic pregnancy
- breast growths that are not cancer
- iron-deficiency anemia
- ovarian cysts
- premenstrual symptoms of depression
- pelvic inflammatory disease

Women also use hormonal BC to treat acne, polycystic ovarian syndrome, pelvic pain caused by endometriosis, bleeding from uterine fibroids, and symptoms of premenstrual dysphoric disorder (PMDD). PMDD is essentially a severe version of PMS, and it affects levels of serotonin in the brain.

How Do You Get Hormonal BC?

If you're sexually active and want hormonal BC, you must go to a healthcare provider who can write you a prescription for it. This usually involves getting a medical exam that will include a pelvic exam and a Pap smear, which is a sample of secretions or cells from the uterus and cervix that's taken to check for cancer. The doctor will also go over your medial history, check your blood pressure, and ask questions about your sexual activity. Some exams are free at health clinics, but they also could cost anywhere from $35 to $250.

In general, parental permission is not needed for prescription methods of birth control. But depending on your state, certain laws can't guarantee that your request for birth control will be completely secret. Confidential services like Planned Parenthood (PP) can help connect you with healthcare providers who will respect your privacy, so if necessary, you can call PP asking for advice on behalf of a friend, then get a referral for yourself. However, you should never, ever take someone else's prescription pills. It's unsafe for you to take them if a doctor isn't aware of your medical history.

How Well Does Hormonal BC Work?

Your odds of getting pregnant on the pill are very low if you take it properly. Less than 1 out of 100 women will get pregnant if they follow the instructions and take it every day exactly as directed. If you don't always take it as directed, your odds of getting pregnant are higher; 8 out of 100 women get pregnant if they do this. Those are also about the same odds for pregnancy when using the ring and patch.

Some factors can lessen the effectiveness of the pill. Two that you may need to worry about are being very overweight and taking certain medications, specifically the antibiotic rifampin and medicine taken orally to treat yeast infections. (Any creams you put in your V-zone won't affect your BC.) Some medicines taken for HIV and to prevent seizures may also make it less effective. St. John's Wort, an herbal supplement commonly used for depression, can also make the pill work less effectively.

Finally, if you vomit or have diarrhea after taking the pill, it may not work. Some girls think it helps to take it at night, but you should ask your healthcare provider for advice and always use a backup method of birth control, such as a condom, in addition to continuing to take the pill.

Cost. Birth control pills will run you about $15–$50 each month, though private health insurers and Medicaid may cover some of this cost.

Other methods may be a bit pricier but even out in the long run: for example, an IUD, which lasts for up to a decade, can cost several hundred dollars for insertion at a doctor's office.

Ease of use. This means not only how easily can you get it—that is, is it available near you or do you have to plan ahead and send away for it through your insurer—but also how it fits into your lifestyle. If the snooze button is your best friend, planning to take a pill in the morning doesn't leave a lot of room for error, but you may not remember it at other times of the day. And the timing really does matter—progestin-only pills have to be taken at the same time every single day.

> **From the frightening-but-true files . . .**
> Half of all unplanned pregnancies among young women are due to birth-control lapses or screwups. And nearly 30 percent of sexually active teens used no birth control during their last sexual encounter.

Also, you need to make sure you can deal with the method's side effects, such as breakthrough bleeding. Even knowing how to properly insert the ring or apply the patch may be too much of a drag for some girls.

What Are the Risks of Hormonal BC?

If you watch enough TV, you've probably memorized the list of possible side effects in some pill commercials. Your doc can fill you in on the big ones for the brand you choose, and it's vital to read the drug reference info that comes with each prescription.

But of the warnings you should really take into account, the biggies are an increased incidence of blood clots, heart attacks, and stroke. If you smoke, however, there's a seriously increased risk of stroke. It's not like you needed another reason to stop smoking, but if you do, this is a damn good one!

Other side effects you might experience include:

- bleeding between periods (most often with progestin-only pills)
- breast tenderness
- nausea and vomiting
- melasma (brown patches on the skin)

What Sex Is Like on the Pill

Many users report their sex drive goes up or down when they start using the pill. Some of this could be mental: you might enjoy having sex more when you're less freaked about the consequences associated with sex; other changes might be physical. Studies do show that the pill can mess with your libido.

The Moral Case Against the Pill

One recent study showed that 13 percent of young people think contraception is morally wrong. Part of this is because not everyone understands how hormonal birth control prevents pregnancy differently than other medications such as the abortion pill. (Maybe that's why, on an episode of *The Simpsons,* Marge Simpson described hormonal BC as "medicine doctors give moms to keep babies up in heaven"!)

Medically speaking, pregnancy is defined as a fertilized egg—

meaning the ovum and sperm coupled up—that has attached itself to the uterine lining. Hormonal birth control, including emergency contraception, prevents eggs from being released, stops sperm from reaching the egg, or doesn't let the fertilized egg implant in your uterus. So sperm and egg actually have to set up residence in Home Sweet Womb to qualify as a pregnancy.

When the pill was developed, some thought it would promote promiscuity and premarital sex. Taking it has nothing to do with whether a woman is slutty. It's more like wearing moisturizer with sunscreen in addition to sunblock if you think you might catch some rays—in other words, it's smart and good for your health.

The more scientifically sound arguments against this type of BC is that it may not be a good idea for everyone to pump their bodies full of hormones. Like any medicine, it comes with risks and side effects, and some people experience mood changes. If you do, changing birth control to a lower level or different combination is what you should request.

What if It Doesn't Work for You?

According to one study, nearly two-thirds of teens did not use a condom the last time they had sex. That's a truly scary statistic, not just because it probably led to unplanned pregnancies and more sexually transmitted infections. It's also a sign that people still aren't getting the message about how effective, cheap, easy to use, and accessible these wondrous little latex tubes are. In fact, 29 percent of young men and 32 percent of young women say that they know little or nothing about condoms. Another study showed that kids ages 15 to 21 who'd had unprotected sex were a lot more likely to believe that condoms reduce sexual pleasure and to be concerned that their partner would not approve of condom use. Attitudes like this lead to a lot of guys getting away with telling some dangerously idiotic lies about condom use. What's worse? You believing them.

But here's the real power of the prophylactic: It's the only type of birth control that can also reduce transmission of STIs. No other method of contraception does it as well—not the pill, a diaphragm, and *especially* not pulling out.

How Sex Feels for Him with a Love Glove

We'll be straight with you: Pretty much no guy wants to wear a rubber. If he's going to get access to a vagina, he's going to want to poke around freely. The uniquely warm, squishy sensation that a guy experiences in vaginal intercourse is a big reason guys have sex in the first place. Putting a latex sheath on it not only takes away that sensation on the surface, but it also constricts the blood vessels, causing some guys to lose sensation. But the bottom line? Sex with a love glove is better than no sex at all. And your stance should be that if he isn't going to wear one, he ain't going to get any. Period.

What Sex with a Condom Is Like for Girls

Believe it or not, it can be great. Despite what you may have heard about the fabulous sensations of barebacking, or not using one, there's less of a difference for women than people claim. It's usually about as pleasurable as unprotected sex for most women, just a little drier, but nothing that some extra lube can't fix. And you'll still feel the thrusts and friction that make your V-zone all tingly.

More important, knowing you're protected will give you the peace of mind to actually *enjoy* the experience. When you're not having visions of babies and viruses tap-dancing through your head, it's much easier to let your mind go and tap into the great physical sensations of sex.

The Cost of Condoms

- Pack of prophylactics: $12
- Bottle of lubrication: $9.
- Knowing you're disease-free and won't be forced to raise a kid when you're still just a kid yourself? *Priceless.*

You're not going to hear this message voiced-over in a TV commercial anytime soon. But condoms offer such an incredible bang for your buck, the advertisement practically writes itself.

On average, a condom in North America costs anywhere from 20¢ to $2.50. How many other things can you buy regularly that give such satisfaction for so few pennies? A can of soda? An app for your phone?

Of course, your partner may balk and say that he's strapped for cash. After you account for shopping, entertainment, car payments, and school, there's not a lot left to go around. Your safety, however, trumps every other expense. If you're choosing not to be abstinent, then condoms are a necessity, not a luxury, for you.

Bust His Condom Myths from A–Z

Whatever a guy's convenient excuse for hating on condoms, you can give him an even better argument for using them: The truth!

Access

Sex may be an "adult" activity, but you don't have to be a certain age to do it more safely. Nationwide, there is no over-18 requirement to purchase condoms at any retailer. No one should refuse the sale of condoms to you if they're on the shelves and available to the rest of the public.

Allergies

Only 1 percent of the general public is allergic to latex, the most common type of condom on the market. Thankfully, polyurethane versions seem to work just fine for those people, and they're as effective as latex. So if your guy claims this malady and isn't open to trying any other type, odds are he's full of crap. Sort it out by asking him to describe the specific symptoms he gets when he's exposed. If he mumbles or avoids answering, it's up to you to decide whether you want to sleep with someone who's willing to put your safety at risk just to preserve his pleasure. (Our take: Ditch him!)

Responsibility and Trust

The tough thing about relying on the male condom as your only method of contraception is that it puts the accountability entirely on the guy. Sad to say, a lot of guys your age don't want or can't handle that responsibility. If you're in the early stages of a relationship with a new guy, hypervigilance about protection could fall annoyingly on your shoulders. You may always be the one who ends up supplying the condoms. You may have to make sure he puts them on perfectly every time. And yes, you may even need to make sure he doesn't secretly remove them during the act. Trust us, it happens!

On top of that, being in a committed relationship has its own set of condom challenges. If you know each other well enough and trust that you're both committed and STI-free, going without a condom starts to look pretty tempting, particularly if you're using hormonal birth control. Guys know that when a girl is less concerned about getting pregnant, she'll be more open to sex without a barrier. Unfortunately, less-than-faithful guys may take advantage of this, creating a false sense of commitment to convince you there's no need for a rubber.

Instead of asking what would make *you* feel most comfortable and secure, he'll start comparing what girls in his past did for him. They loved him enough to get on birth control, or they wanted to show their faithfulness by going without condoms. After all, if you can't get pregnant thanks to the pill, then the only reason to wear one would be if you're at risk of getting an STI from someone else. He swears up and down that he's totally clean and only having sex with you . . . so *you* must be the shady one with something to hide. His last girlfriend proved herself to him—why can't you?

This is some backwards logic, and a guy who uses it on you is serving one person: himself. He's not looking for a closer connection. He's breaking you down, making you doubt yourself, and feel paranoid or stupid for not surrendering your trust. These are all manipulative things. All so that he can get off a little easier.

Don't let a guy convince you to go against all you know is true about sex and protection just because he's dangling a commitment in front of you.

Strength

Before condoms can be sold in North America, they have to meet certain government standards. Companies must put their products through rigorous testing, mostly stuff that a human penis could never hope to replicate.

For the most part, your average rubber passes with flying colors. Still, they are not indestructible. But that's no excuse to forgo protection. If a guy claims he can't use them because they break more often than that for him, he's probably not using them correctly. Let him know that a few drops of water or silicone-based lubricant (never any that contain oil) on both the inside and exterior of the condom can help prevent friction that leads to tearing.

Be a Condom Connoisseur

Among the things that every smart girl should be able to do—build a fire, change a flat tire, sweet-talk your way into the VIP line or out of a speeding ticket—knowing how to properly use a condom tops the list. Clearly, it's a skill that's sorely lacking: One recent study showed that nearly one in three teens who used a condom put it on too late, and about 10 percent removed it too soon.

Here's a step-by-step tutorial on doing it right. Don't just memorize it. Go ahead and test it yourself with a pack of prophylactics and a banana, cucumber, or an anatomically correct dildo or vibrator. The more comfortable you feel putting a sack on a stand-in, the easier things will go when you're face to face with the real thing.

Before You Get Busy . . .

• Make sure you have plenty of condoms on hand—at least two for each sex session just in case one breaks or falls off.

- Keep the condoms away from heat and excessive light. That means far from bedside tables near radiators, sunny windowsills, and toasty car glove compartments. And never use a condom that's been in a wallet or pocket for a while. The friction from sitting on it and rubbing it against other items can wear down the latex, making it more susceptible to tears. (The "lucky" rubber he's been carting around in his jeans since seventh grade won't cut it.)
- Make sure the condom is well within its expiration date, which should be located on the box and on the wrapper. If it's not visible or if you can't read it, find one that's clearly marked. Otherwise, the condom may crack or tear because latex dries out over time.

Just Before the Action Starts . . .

- We've heard stories about girls trying to rip rubber packages open with their teeth. Easy tiger! Sexy, it's not. Plus, you can tear the latex with your pearly whites. Open a condom wrapper with your hands only, using the fleshy pads of your fingers to push it out. Be careful, too, that you don't snag a fingernail, piercing, or other jewelry on it.
- Once you open the package, do a quick check of the latex. Seem too sticky or brittle? Toss it and find another. The consistency should be smooth and a little moist.
- Most condoms have a reservoir tip, a small bubble on top that gives it the look of a hat. This helps catch the semen, but it involves a little prep work. Before you roll the condom on the penis, you need to pinch the tip of it to get rid of any excess air so it's less likely to burst. Then, place it on so it fits snugly against the head of the penis.

- Roll the condom down toward the base of the shaft, making sure it's completely unfurled and that the majority of his penis is covered. There should be a little room left at the tip, about a half an inch or so, and the open end should sit nice and tight around the base of the penis. If it doesn't look that way or you think it's inside out, throw it away and try again with a new condom.

During the Act . . .

- Using a lubricant with condoms can make the sensations of sex more pleasurable for you both. But—and this is a big but—it has to be the right kind. You need to stick to water-based fluids (you'll find them under brand names like Astroglide). Other substances actually break down the latex: Never use shortening (e.g., Crisco), lotions, petroleum jelly (Vaseline), or baby oil. You can put the water-based lube near your vulva, on the outside of the condom, or a drop or two inside the condom before he puts it on.
- Keep an eye on his penis throughout your encounter to make sure the condom is firmly in place. It's a good idea to pay attention to the sensation of what the rubber feels like inside you so that you'll know if anything changes, whether it falls off, breaks, or he removes it.

After the Deed Is Done . . .

- Remove the condom right after he ejaculates, while he's still a little hard. Your dude shouldn't keep thrusting into you after he comes because he'll get softer and smaller, which means there's more opportunity for the condom to come off. One of you should grasp the condom at the base of the penis and slide it off carefully, making sure all the semen stays inside.

- It's a good idea to tie off the end of the condom so that fluids don't leak out and create a health risk for anyone.
- Have the guy go wash up immediately after intercourse, making sure he cleans his penis thoroughly before he comes back to you. If you're still nekkid, there's no reason to risk accidentally getting any spunk near you after you've gone to so much trouble to keep it out in the first place.

Propo No-Nos

Now that you know the drill, be aware of these common condom mistakes you should never, ever make.

- Don't double bag it. It actually makes it prone to tearing as the two layers rub against each other.
- Don't let him take the condom off after he comes and then re-enter you, or put his penis near the entrance of your vagina. Sperm can live outside the body if they're in an environment that's warm and moist. Like the one between your legs, for instance. They'll like the neighborhood so much, they may even try to relocate into a spacious new home on Uterus Lane, a cute one egg with plenty of room for a baby.
- Don't use it twice. Each condom is built for one use and one use only. Any more and you risk stressing the latex beyond its capacity. And definitely don't turn it inside out

and use it. No matter what he says, it's not the same thing as wearing your underwear wrong side out on laundry day. Gross, yes, but definitely not harmless.

- Don't let him have anal sex with you and then put his penis in your vagina while he's wearing a condom. Alternating between vaginal and then anal sex can easily transfer bacteria that creates nasty vaginal infections. You need a new condom every time you do something new after anal sex.
- Don't cut the condom because he's smaller than the size of the one you have on hand. A condom can't work unless it fits tight around the base of his penis. It does this with the help of the ring at the opening, so you can't remove it. Instead, shop for a shorter size.
- Don't have sex without a backup condom. In the event of breakage or slippage, some people can't resist just finishing the deed anyway, even if they know it's not right, because they're just too turned on. Don't be one of them.
- Don't use anything that's not a condom and think it will work like one. Boxer shorts and plastic baggies are not effective barriers!

Nookie 911: How to Deal with Condom Emergencies

Accidents happen, but they don't have to end in disaster if you know what to do in these three familiar situations.

Scenario 1: It Fell Off Inside You

The cause: He got limp, he thrust too hard, or it slipped.

Scenario 2: It Broke

The cause: Too much friction, not enough lubrication, or using a sub-par condom.

Scenario 3: You're Not Sure if He Had it on the Whole Time

The cause: You didn't see it on him when he entered you, he said it was on but took it off part of the way through, or you couldn't find it afterward.

The solution: For all of the above, you need to consider emergency contraception or EC (also known as the morning after pill) as your first line of defense against unwanted pregnancy. This is especially crucial if you know that he came inside you, and it's critical to do it ASAP.

The most popular emergency contraception method is named Plan B. It's a hormonal contraceptive, similar to a high dose of the birth control pill, that can be taken up to five days after you have unprotected sex to reduce the risk of pregnancy. We strongly recommend that you always have a full dose on hand if you're sexually active, just in case you can't get it within the five-day period following a potential accident or session where you didn't use protection.

The best time to take it is immediately after the sex happens. You can take it within five days of unprotected sex, but it's best if you do it within 24 hours (there's a 95 percent effectiveness rate). It's 89 percent effective if you take it within 72 hours (three days) and drops to 75 percent effective if you take it within 120 hours (five days).

Plan B is available without a prescription if you're 17 and over; if you're younger, you need a prescription to obtain it, which may require a medical checkup first. Since you never know where you'll be when you need it, get one from your doctor and keep it close at hand in the event of an emergency.

👍 What to **SAY** to His **LIES**:

✓ "I read about a new size/style of condom that seems to be made for your body. Let's try it."

✓ "I do love you—and since I know you love me too, you won't question my need to 'feel safe.'"

✓ "I know how to put it on. Here, watch. . . ."

✓ "You hate condoms, huh? Well, I really hate the idea of getting pregnant."

✓ "I get that you have an issue with buying condoms in public. I don't like having strangers know about my sex life either. But asking a cashier for them is a lot easier than explaining to our parents that you got me pregnant."

✓ "I'm sure I'm clean, but many STIs don't have symptoms. I care about you and myself, so I want to make sure we're both protected."

✓ "You have two choices: sex with a condom, or none at all. What'll it be?"

✓ "I can't believe other girls let you get away with that. Aren't you glad you're with someone smarter now?"

☞ What to **DO** if You Already Bought the **LIE:**

You can't redo the past, but you can control the future. So from this moment forward, insist on wearing a condom, and use it correctly every time. Remind the guy that every single time you have sex, you have a choice—how, where, when, and who to do it with. It doesn't matter what you did before. And newsflash: He **still** gets to have sex! With you! Dude should be down on his knees thanking God he's doing it with someone smart and caring enough to protect **both** of you.

✓ "We might have been fortunate before. But if you want to get lucky tonight and from here on out, it's only going to happen if you wear a condom."

✓ "It only takes one sperm to mess up all our plans, and 300 million of them end up inside me when we have sex even one time without a condom. I don't like those odds, so I'm not going to play them ever again."

✓ "I don't care what we did before or what other girls did. This is what you need to do if you want to continue to be with me here and now."

✓ "It freaks me out how close we could have come to having something bad happen. So if you want me to feel more comfortable and relaxed enough to have sex, then we have to use a condom."

✓ "I learned a little bit more about how risky having sex without a condom really is, so I decided that I'm not going to have sex ever again without a condom until I'm ready to deal with consequences like having a baby."

Q&A

Q: My boyfriend said his ex "went crazy" on the pill and doesn't want me to take it. Will that happen to me?

A: There's no way of knowing what BC she took or what kind of mental health history she had before going on it that could have contributed to this. Mood swings are a possibility, but everyone responds to each method differently.

Q: I heard the pill helps clear up acne, but my boyfriend says it's actually having sex that does it. Who's right?

A: If he were correct, wouldn't the condom companies have put half of the beauty industry out of business by now? Teens everywhere would have flawless skin overnight! Your skin tends to grow out of its pimply phase around age 18—coincidentally, when a lot of people have sex for the first time and also when many girls start combined hormone methods that help the skin. But no, it is not the sex.

Q: I know guys like super-thin condoms, but aren't they more prone to breakage? How do I know what's a quality one and what isn't?

A: It sounds counterintuitive, but thinner is actually better. Poor quality condoms tend to be made of thicker, less flexible material, so there's less give and more opportunities to tear when its durability is put to the test.

As you shop around, it's wise to do your own research, too. Start with consumer organizations like Consumer Reports, which does its own independent testing of condoms. Their most recent studies found that the Night Light glow-in-the-dark model had poor marks for strength and leakage; one of the most reliable was Trojan Her Pleasure Ecstasy.

Q: **My guy stays hard up until the point we try to put the condom on, then loses his erection. Is that normal?**

A: Totally. One of the main complaints guys and girls share about condoms is that it takes the fun out of foreplay. In fact, a guy who's all pumped up may get a flat tire just at the sight of a condom. It doesn't mean he can't perform or isn't attracted to you. It could easily be a mental block that comes from experience—or, more likely, lack of it.

Q: **Do condoms work in hot tubs?**

A: Among the problems with hot tub love is the high chance water will seep into the condom, creating slippage. That can be hard to detect when a guy is going from one warm, wet environment (the tub) to another (your V-zone). Any natural lubrication you have or that's on the condom will wash off quickly, making for a less comfy ride with more friction—and more opportunity to tear—than you'd have on land.

And while most guys stay hard in warm water, remember that if he rises out into the cold air, the dastardly phenomenon known as shrinkage can occur. Then it's bye-bye Mr. Jimmyhat.

There are also specific environmental challenges. When condoms are put through rigorous testing before they can be sold, hot tubs are *not* one of the places they're tried out. There's a reason for that. It's thought that exposure to heat and chemicals like chlorine and ozone may weaken the latex; how exactly that plays out in the bubbly environment isn't clear. And if you've been sunning, any lotions or oils you put on your body could weaken the material as well. (Another good reason to avoid hot tub love: Thrusting motions can force microbes into the vaginal canal, which can lead to infection. And if the tub is not properly chlorinated, it may actually change the pH levels of your body, putting you at risk for a yeast infection).

Still, it's better than bareback. If you absolutely must have sex, you need to wear a condom and have an extra on hand if it breaks. Make sure you put it on before you enter the tub, and take it out immediately after use. Souvenirs of your romp are not appreciated by others.

Oh, and just a reminder: sex is illegal in public places like beaches, pools, lakes, and rivers. You don't want to know how handcuffs feel when applied to a naked, sunburned body.

Q: **Is there such a thing as a female condom (FC)?**

A: A lot of people think the FC is on a par with the unicorn—just a figment of the imagination. It does indeed exist and it may be a good option for you. It's not to be confused, however, with the dental dam.

The female condom is a sheath of latex or polyurethane that goes in the vagina (or anus) and provides a tube-shaped barrier between your lady parts and his penis. Some women like it because it puts responsibility for protection in their hands and it doesn't mess with your hormones. And unlike male condoms that require a guy to be erect to be put on, you can plan much further ahead with an FC—leaving it inserted up to 8 hours is okay.

They're between 75 and 82 percent effective at preventing STIs and pregnancy, according to the National Institutes of Health. So with pretty decent protection odds, how come you don't hear more about it?

The issue is that the girl version is even trickier to master than the male one. You start by squeezing the closed end of the tube between your thumb and forefinger, then insert it all the way in to the vagina so that it can't fall out. Finding out where exactly that is for you can take a little trial and error and might require using a tampon or dildo to test. Once you release it inside you, you put your index finger in and press it up so that the latex touches your cervix. That will leave you with about an inch of the material hanging out from your vulva. Once you're ready to have sex, you or your guy will need to guide his penis into you to make sure it's covered by the sheath.

Removing it after the deed presents its own challenges. You grasp the condom and squeeze your thumb and index finger together, twisting off the open end of the condom so no ejaculate will leak out. That requires a steady hand and a meticulous nature, something not everyone has. Oh, and you had better be okay with some goofy noises during intercourse. You might find its squeaky-dog-toy soundtrack off-putting, but a little lube should take care of the auditory accompaniment.

Q: **Does using spermicide help or hurt your body? I'm freaked about putting chemicals near my sensitive parts.**

A: You're right to be concerned. The most commonly used spermicide, Nonoxynol 9, used to be a staple in condoms. Then it was found that the substance causes skin abrasions and irritates the lining of the vagina, actually leading to an increased risk of HIV transmission. Today, the Centers For Disease Control no longer recommends its use, especially if your primary goal is to protect yourself from STIs.

LIE #9

"That bump has always been there."

PROTECTING YOURSELF FROM STIS, PLAYERS, AND OTHER STUFF THAT CREEPS YOU OUT

🐴 Other Ways He **MIGHT** Say It

✗ "Of course I'm clean, trust me."

✗ "If you think there's something wrong with me, it must be because you gave it to me."

✗ "STIs aren't a big deal. You just take some medicine and you're cured."

✗ "I can't afford to get tested."

✗ "If you have an STI, you're a slut."

✗ "You probably got it from a toilet seat, not me."

✗ "You deserve an STI if you sleep around."

✗ "If I shave my balls I can't get an STI."

✗ "Oral sex is 100 percent safe."

☞ The **TRUTH**:

You know you're supposed to have "the talk" with every
guy about his STI status before clothes come off and libidos
turn on. But you can't underestimate the power that raging
hormones and a ridonkulously hot guy will have to cancel any
sexual health summit meeting you planned. Sometimes it's
just too easy to chicken out—you're embarrassed to bring it up
or afraid of offending him. Or other things "just happen" in a
dark basement or backseat of a car the moment you open
your lips for the chat.

We don't care how amazingly connected you feel to a guy.
If you cannot talk to him about STIs, **you cannot have sex
with him**. No ifs or ands, and certainly no buts. STIs are real,
dangerous, and the risk of catching them is serious every
time you're together, even the first.

What Are Your Odds
of Getting an STI, Really?

Since you probably don't know many people with life-threaten-
ing STIs like HIV, you may not think they're a serious risk for you.
But that could be a fatal assumption.

There's no use in beating around the bush: One in four teens—
that goes for all of them, including your BFFs, fremenies, crushes,

and acquaintances—has had a sexually transmitted infection. About half of all new HIV infections occur in people under age 25.

If that doesn't give you pause, know that the numbers are getting worse. Although young people ages 15 to 24 make up only one quarter of the population of people who are sexually active, they acquire half of new STIs. Girls in particular are at higher risk: females ages 15 to 19 have the most chlamydia and gonorrhea cases of any age group.

It's easier for girls to get almost every type of STI. One reason you're at greater risk is that the lining of your cervix doesn't become fully mature until your late teens, and less-developed tissue makes you more prone to infection from STIs.

Just What Is an STI?

There are many types of sexually transmitted infections. They can be broken down into two general categories, viral and bacterial, depending on what type of microorganism is the culprit. The bacterial kind—for example, chlamydia, gonorrhea, and syphilis—can be cured with the use of antibiotics. Viral STIs, however, are caused by viruses and in most cases can only be treated, not cured. Examples of viral infections you can have for life are HIV, human papillomavirus (HPV), herpes, and hepatitis B.

One other category to be aware of are STIs caused by protozoa, such as trichomoniasis, or other organisms like crabs, scabies, and pubic lice, which can be cured with the use of antibiotics or topical creams and lotions.

"But Everyone Gets Them" and
Other Coital Cop-Outs

Cervical cancer, for example, causes more deaths than HIV in women, but both should be taken equally seriously. If not properly treated, chlamydia and gonorrhea can lead to pelvic inflammatory disease. That's a painful condition with effects like scarring of reproductive organs that can lead to pregnancy complications, miscarriages, or the inability to ever have a baby.

The human papillomavirus (HPV) can be transmitted through genital contact without intercourse. That's right—even through oral sex or a hand job. And many carriers have no symptoms at all. Thirty of the more than 100 strains of HPV can lead to cervical, penile, and anal cancers.

The Moral Behind Oral

EVER THOUGHT THAT the really seriously bad stuff can't be transferred through oral? You're dead wrong. While the risk of getting HIV or another STI is higher with unprotected anal or vaginal intercourse, you can still get them orally.

That means just having the penis in your mouth or being exposed to sperm can also expose you to an STI. And the oral friction contact between you and his penis can transmit syphilis and herpes. Many studies have also shown that HPV is linked to throat cancers in people who regularly engaged in unprotected oral. And a new study found that women who've had six or more oral sex partners are more likely to get oral cancer.

Don't forget that even just the tip of the penis counts. Preejaculate contains just as many pathogens—that is, bacteria and viruses—as semen.

The "Perfect" Privates: What His Anatomy Says about His Risk

The short answer? Very little. Lack of obvious symptoms says nothing about what's really going on there. In fact, it's more likely for guys to be asymptomatic—that is, have no visible or physiological signs and still have STIs.

In general, the skin around a guy's genital area should be smooth and even-toned, and not red, discolored, or irritated. If the boy was not circumcised, the foreskin can be slightly darker, but it should not be textured or bumpy, or appear to have any sort of lesions. Some types of bumps crop up during an outbreak of an STI, such as herpes, when the infection is active, but although they can disappear days or weeks later, you can still get infected.

While some bumps are just benign cysts or shiny raised areas around the head of the penis known as pearly penile papules, you can't tell which ones are okay and which ones are not.

"Only Sluts Get Diseases" and Other Nasty Nonsense

Reality check: A person who has an STI will not "look dirty" on the outside. The valedictorian and the "player" alike could be carrying an STI. The number of partners you've had may raise your personal risk, but it is not a slam-dunk predictor. Nevertheless, talking with your partner about your sexual history may actually help you become closer as a couple. A recent study of guys and girls ages 15 to 24 in England found that talking about sexual history was a better sign of a relationship getting serious than meeting the person's parents. The cool part about this? It means more people are valuing openness about sexual health as a factor for relationship potential!

When Do I Need to Go to the Gyno and Get Tested?

Teen girls typically wait to seek health care an average of 12 months after becoming sexually active. That's way too long to go unchecked and uninformed.

As for routine sexual health testing, you should get your first Pap smear at 18 if you're not sexually active. But remember, active means the whole range of stuff we discussed in the first chapter—even just genital touching. You should get a Pap annually if you're sexually active and get tested every 6 to 12 months or when you have a new sex partner.

In the meantime, monitor your own body, particularly your V-zone, for unusual smells, bumps, warts, secretions, cuts, or anything else that looks funky. Don't be afraid to have it checked and have it be nothing but a pimple—that's a good thing! But if you have any of the following signs and are sexually active, you must get checked by a doctor ASAP.

- Vaginal or genital swelling
- Difficult or frequent urination
- A rash on the genitals accompanied by a sore throat with no other symptoms of a cold
- Bleeding that occurs when you're not menstruating or when you have sex
- Burning or itching sensations on your vulva or in your vagina
- Pelvic pain

Getting evaluated is a must, but it doesn't have to be by your longtime pediatrician or cost you an arm and a leg. Check your area or college campus for reproductive health care clinics that do testing. Costs for STD testing and services may vary from clinic to clinic, and some are free or low cost. One great new mobile service lets you text your zip code to GYTNOW (498669) to get info about nearby testing centers.

If you're underage, you can usually get testing and treatment without parental consent, though it may be necessary in some cases if you're under 14. Do know, however, that some states will allow healthcare providers to release results or treatment info to your parents. Ask ahead of time if your appointment and records will be confidential.

What to Expect During an STI Exam

Your first visit can be a bit intimidating, but it's easy to get through if you bring a friend, family member, or your partner.

A pelvic exam is nothing like sex. And if you feel awkward, you may forget to ask about things on your mind, like whether treatments will affect any other drugs, vitamins, or supplements you take. Make a list of your questions in advance. You will be asked the following:

- How many partners you've had in the past few months and over your lifetime
- What kinds of sex you have (e.g., oral, anal, vaginal) and if you use condoms
- Whether you have sex with women, men, or both
- The start date of your last period

- If you've had an STI in the past and what symptoms you
  had at the time
- If you use drugs or alcohol
- What medications you've used to treat past infections, what
  prescriptions and vitamins you currently take, and if you're
  allergic to any drugs

You must answer every question truthfully, even if it embar-
rasses you, so that you can get the most thorough treatment
possible. It's also smart to ask about the infections you will get
tested for, so you can make sure herpes and HIV are covered.
Just because your blood is drawn or a urine or tissue cell sample
is taken, you can't assume they're being tested for all STIs. You
may need to make a special request to have the full range offered.

Sometimes a diagnosis can be made on the spot and treatment
prescribed at that moment. Other times, your healthcare provider
may need to send a sample away to a lab, which may take two
weeks to return results. Either way, you have to follow up, not
assume that no news is good news. You also need to refrain from
sexual activity until the test results are back.

When the Results Are In

When you get the news, your healthcare provider will counsel
you about your treatment options. Remember, all STIs, including
HIV, are treatable, and some, like chlamydia and gonorrhea, are
curable.

Getting a positive diagnosis is a hard thing to deal with. You
might feel bad about yourself. But remember, an STI is not "proof
of sluttiness" or a penalty you deserve for having premarital sex.

You don't need to tell friends or family about it if you don't want to, but it is a good idea to ask your healthcare provider for a referral to a therapist or counselor. The next most important call you need to make is to your partner or partners. Even if you hate their guts or don't know which one gave it to you, it's not your job to decide whether someone who might have an STI goes untreated.

When you talk to him, be prepared for him to be upset—you would be, too. The natural reaction is to feel fear, even disgust. Let him know you're telling him because you care about his health. It may be the last time you ever talk, but at least you'll have acted responsibly.

Sexual Responsibility: What to Do

If having sex is all about thinking about what feels good in the short-term, taking sexual responsibility is training yourself to think long-term. How will it feel if you get something incurable from a five-minute activity with a guy you're not sure is STI-free? Will the pain, bumps, itching, or embarrassment that result be worth it if you get something incurable? Even if it means irritating a guy who thinks you don't trust him by asking his status, that's the only real way you can protect your health and safety, in addition to practicing safer sex.

Anytime a guy tells you that "that bump's always been there," you cannot have any type of sexual contact with him—not even a hand job—until a doctor determines what it really is. If he ignores it, he not only is trying to minimize the importance of his own sexual health, he is also minimizing the importance of your safety. Forget the "you have to believe me!" crap. Take his response as a good reason to think he may be hiding something.

Remember, there's no way of knowing if a guy is clean or how many people he has slept with—anyone can lie. Even only one person means nothing, because that person could have had many partners. And don't buy into excuses like he's too young, too smart, or too careful to have picked up something.

Deciding whether to take a guy's word for it is tricky. You *can* ask to see his paperwork. It may seem excessive, but if there's a voice in the back of your mind that makes you wonder if he might not be 100 percent straight, listen to it and require whatever proof you need.

When you are ready to have sex, you know the drill: Use a condom. That means his *entire* penis should be covered. If it's not and you find yourself face-to-face with an odd bump or lesion, don't ask him what it is, how long it's been there, or how he got it. Just put your clothes back on and head for the door. And if a guy refuses to get tested, break it off with him. Urging him to care for himself by walking away might be just the thing he needs to get him on track. But that's not something you need to wait around for.

👍 What to **SAY** to His **LIES**:

✓ "I don't do anything that's not safe. Having any sort of sexual contact that's not protected isn't safe."

✓ "Neither one of us is a doctor, so we can't say for sure. Until you've been tested, it's not smart for either of us to take a chance."

✓ "You might be worried that I think something bad about you or your past if I insist on testing. But it makes me like you more when you protect me."

✓ "I realize that you may think you haven't slept around enough to get an STI. I'm pretty new to it, too, which is why I don't want to take any chances."

✓ "It doesn't matter if the last girl you were with looked clean. She might have symptoms and not know it. Same for me, and I could be giving it to you if we don't use a condom."

✓ "I don't need to tell you how many people I've been with. All you need to know is that I'm always safe."

✓ "Having an STI has nothing to do with sluttiness or being dirty. Anyone can get one from skin-on-skin contact."

✓ "I know we're in a committed relationship, but our health is even more important than trust. If you really love or care for me, you have to get that bump checked out before we do more."

☞ What to **DO** if You Already Bought the **LIE:**

Tell your guy to keep his pants on until he's got the paperwork to prove he's STI-free. Nothing's a better motivator to get a guy to head to the doc than the thought of going without sex from you! Boys and men of all ages are more likely to ignore symptoms or even pain far longer then women and girls, so whatever the incentive, it's fine if it works.

If you're under the impression that an STI reflects on character, consider that a married woman who's never slept with anyone but her husband (and not even until her wedding night) could get herpes if her husband cheats with an infected partner. Be sympathetic if you are the one getting told that your partner has found out he has an STI.

Q&A

Q: I found a new bump. What is it? I'm scared to get tested. What if I find out I have something?

A: Bumps on women are harder to gauge because women have unique vaginas and vulvas that are all different shapes ands sizes. The size of the labia majora or minora can have wrinkles and folds. No two vaginas look alike! If you have a bump that worries you, don't pick or poke at it. It may be something minor, like a rash, allergic reaction, ingrown hair, or blemish due to sweat. But don't just ignore it and hope it goes away! You must get it checked out by a pro in case you need treatment.

Q: Is it true you can get an STI from a toilet seat?

A: Not unless you were eating off of it. This may gross you out, but the only STI commonly found in bathrooms is hepatitis A, and that's transmitted by feces-mouth contact. Pubic lice used to be a bigger issue, but because so many people wax and shave their privates it's prevalence in the general population is way down.

Q: My guy's semen has started to sort of itch when I'm in contact with it. Does that mean it's an STI?

A: Actually, it's more likely that you have an allergy to it. Reactions include pain, itching, redness, and swelling, or hives. But don't worry; it has nothing to do with whether you guys are meant for each other romantically.

Q: I'm hearing a lot about the HPV vaccine. Do I have to get it?

A: It's a good idea. There are two of them, Cervarix and Gardasil, that protect against the strains of HPV that cause 70 percent of cervical cancer cases for women ages 9 to 26. They're administered around age 11 or 12 before you're sexually active because it provides better protection the earlier you get it.

LIE #10

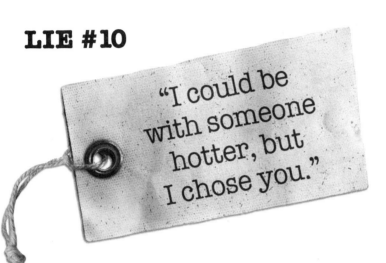

"I could be with someone hotter, but I chose you."

HOW TO MAKE PEACE WITH YOURSELF FROM HEAD TO TOE AND DECLARE WAR ON BODY HATE

🐾 Other Ways He **MIGHT** Say It

✗ "You're too fat/skinny/ugly for anyone else to be with you."

✗ "You have weird feet/knees, but I still love you."

✗ "You're lucky to be with me—no one else would want someone who looks like you."

✗ "Your boobs look weird."

✗ "There's something wrong with your vagina."

✗ "Your vadge is dirty. You need to douche."

✗ "It's not like you could do any better than me."

☞ The **TRUTH**:

Taking aim at your body is one of the cheapest shots a guy can level at you. It's also one of the most devastating. Even whip-smart, stop-and-stare beautiful women who know better than to let themselves be judged can crumble when someone verbally assaults their physique, from their freckles to their stretch marks.

Most boys know better than dare to criticize a girl's body if they care about her. But some guys use these underhanded comments as a control tactic. Acting as if no one else would want you because of this flaw or that, a guy automatically casts himself as a prince among men for tolerating being seen with you or accepting a loser like you.

Some assholes actively sniff out your greatest perceived weakness and use it against you. ("You're right. You could stand to lose a few pounds.") Often they have to invent one you didn't know you had ("What, no one told you that you have a hook nose before? I'm surprised. I mean, it's fine with me but. . . .")

Other guys put you down more subtly by flipping one of your flaws into something they alone love, making you dependent on them for reassurance. ("Stop talking about your pooch. You're lucky I have a thing for girls with a little meat on their bones.") Or they target your most feminine parts, like your breasts or vagina, and wonder out loud why they don't look like the ones they see in porn, which represent absurd standards few women can achieve without surgery.

The overall effect of such criticism is to make you feel deficient. And when a guy preys on your insecurities this way, it exposes him as an abusive person.

Mr. Wrong Meets Miss Congeniality

By age 13, 53 percent of American girls say they're unhappy with their bodies. When they get to age 17, this number grows to 78 percent. A majority of girls feel some sense of body shame, and that sets them up to have a bad body image and low self-esteem. As a result, they place a skewed amount of importance on looks or sex in a relationship.

Even if you know better than to be appreciated for only your body—or to believe that the text "Babe ur so hott" is a sonnet to your beauty—it's nice to feel close to someone and hope that they see a little bit of a swan beneath what you think is an ugly duckling exterior. That can make you excuse a lot of other bad behaviors—cheating, lying, even physical abuse—as long as there are moments you feel special.

Of course, we don't need a guy's love to transform us into something beautiful. We show up every day trying to look like the "after" shot of a beauty makeover. We do this by spending billions annually on miracle serums, antifrizz potions, and the perfect shade of lip-gloss just to look "naturally beautiful." (As if the natural you were born with could be improved upon.) We're taught pretty early on by the beauty industry and other businesses that it's important to spend money to look good for other people—that by being an object of affection for someone else, we can get self-worth. That idea doesn't just come from looking up to Disney princesses or playing with hypersexualized Bratz dolls. Lots of parents also reinforce the idea that girls just need to be pretty, not smart or funny, to make it in the world. Studies show that parents actually take better care of attractive children, making them wear seatbelts or avoid dangerous activities, than they do of their ugly ones.

Believe it or not, there was a time when you were supposed to be gawky, awkward, and a little rough around the edges as a teen. The whole idea was to use this time to slowly come into your own, not arrive looking camera-ready. Part of the fun was knowing you would look back at hilarious cringe-worthy chronicles of how far you had come. Now we have scores of photos that had to be reshot digitally seven times to get the perfect "candid" pic. Whether we like it or not, we're all operating under a big beauty lie forced on us by the media, then perpetuated by our insecurities. By the time you reach 17, you will have received over 250,000 commercial messages, many of them promoting the current standard of beauty as blonde, thin, curvy, fit, and tan. We've become a society that values impossibly huge curves (Kim Kardashian's rear) and straight lines (Blake Lively's willowy physique) at the same time.

We also don't even know what "hot" really looks like anymore, because nearly every commercial image is Photoshopped, trimmed, and skimmed before it gets to us. A cover shot of a model or movie star may be a composite of different people's body parts with the celeb's head on top. Society goes to many extremes to sell clothing, including making women feel they have be dangerously thin to set foot on a runway. (The average female model weighs up to 25 percent less than the typical woman and maintains her weight at about 15 to 20 percent below what is considered healthy for her age and height.)

There is a lot of pressure to be a walking coat hanger, but not as much as trying to do that *and* make good grades, get noticed by guys at school (but not too much—you don't want to make them think you're desperate for attention!), deal with friends' dramas, and be a good daughter every day. Face it, *you're* always under the lights, too. Every moment of your life is played out on a screen, whether it's videophone, digital camera, computer, or TV. It's documented and dissected, so you have to spend hours perfecting the cutesy-sexy-tough face that makes the best impression. Rebellion against the norm has to be calculated too. It can't be too over the top, Lady Gaga-style, because even that goes mainstream eventually. And if you're just trying to be yourself while everyone else attempts to be someone else's idea of hot, you better not look as if you care too much. Then you run the risk of getting the worst name of all: "fake."

It's such a razor-thin line of perfection girls must walk, it's surprising that young women have a shred of self-worth or a dollar left trying to keep up. No matter how much energy you put into looking like a star—be it rock, porn, movie, or runway—you have no guarantee you'll be liked any more by a guy because of it. He might have even preferred the original you to the unrecognizable version that's here now.

How Much Do Looks Really Matter?

Studies show that regardless of gender, people with similar levels of physical attractiveness tend to date each other, with more attractive people being more particular about the physical attractiveness of their potential dates. But before you go busting your ass for a six-pack, here's the great part: Beauty really is in the eye of the beholder and it has a lot to do with where you live. So in certain communities, you don't have to keep up with the scary celeb ideal at all. Some men are more prone to be interested in what's real: a bit of a belly or some junk in the trunk. And some men don't notice when your breasts jiggle "too much." They think, *Boobs! Holy crap! I can't believe I'm seeing boobs!* And on the whole, studies show that men rate women who look confident as more attractive.

Still, there are some particular body issues you really are sensitive about: your vagina, your breasts, and your weight. Here's why what you think about each one can affect how you interact with guys.

Looking at the V-zone

Ever heard a guy say something like, "Ugh, vaginas are ugly"? Well, he's wrong.

For some reason, guys from your biology class to Hollywood think it's open season on this part of your anatomy. It's not as if you needed help to feel worse about your vadge. One study found that 9 out of 10 women feel some shame when talking about their vaginas.

Confusion about even simple mechanics leads people to make up silly terms that sound like baby talk (hoo-hoo, chichi), or names you'd give a house pet (honeypot, pussy), or bad directions (down there, down south). Worse, other people cringe around the word "vagina" or even say things like "Ugh, don't use that word—it's dirty."

Let's get it straight: Your lady parts are a collection of delicate tissues and organs, each one built in a particular way to make you happy and healthy. Collectively, the ones you see on the outside are called the vulva, which is made up of the mons pubis, labia, clitoris, urethra, perineum, and anus. Check them out with a hand mirror so you can see what each one looks like.

You're probably wondering if yours are normal. So does everyone else . . . but that's where the similarities between you and other

people end when it comes to the vagina. Here are some ways they
can vary.

Size and Shape

Most vaginas are between four and seven inches in length. And
the width changes based on what's inside there. Otherwise, the
walls are in contact with each other. Don't even think of it like a
hole—it only becomes one when it accommodates a tampon or
a penis.

Folded over the entrance to your vagina are your labia majora,
or outer lips. These are the fleshy flaps of skin that are usually
covered with hair. They get engorged with blood, usually darken-
ing their appearance, and expand when you get turned on. But
often the inner ones, the labia minora, are longer or more promi-
nent so it's a misleading name. One thing they all have in common
is that they're hairless and contain glands that secrete sebum, a
moist substance that helps facilitate sex.

One size issue that you may worry about: There's a perception
that guys can tell how much sex you've had or think you're cheating on them if you're "loose down there." That's totally ridiculous
and untrue. The only thing that can influence your tightness at
this age is vaginal childbirth. Your size is just the way you were
built. And maybe anyone judging you on yours is insecure about
how *they* were designed.

Color

Forget the name "pink taco." Not all vaginal lips are pink,
which should be very obvious when normal skin color varies
within all the Crayola rainbow options. That means that purplish
on a white girl, dark or nearly black on a Latina, and peach on a

mixed race girl are all fine. While they may look flushed when you're sexually roused, like your cheeks or chest might during a workout, this color is different for everyone. Whatever yours is, it's absolutely fine.

Skin Texture

Smoothness of both the inner and outer vaginal tissue varies. Inside the vaginal canal, it's likely ribbed or rippled—so that your vagina can expand to take in a penis or let a baby out. Your vagina is particularly ridged at the front. Feel free to explore with clean fingers to see what we mean.

Smell and Taste

When all is well down there, you might have a slight musky smell. This scent varies over the course of the month. The things that throw scent off are medications, menstruation, or infections.

Discharge

The vagina is a self-cleaning oven! Your body secretes fluids that can be thin, sticky, and elastic or thick and gooey. Typically, these fluids are clear, white, or off-white in color. The mucus, or "discharge" from your vagina, which you'll sometimes see on your underwear, may vary in texture, scent, and color. This could freak you out, but it keeps your vagina clean of bacteria and maintains a careful acid balance (or pH) vital to your health. Any changes could actually be an early warning that you need treatment for a health issue.

Hair

Your muff fluff depends on factors like your ethnic heritage and hormones. But it was put there to keep your vagina safe and clean. It keeps out bacteria and transmits pheromones—natural chemicals sensed by the brain through your nose that attract guys. It can extend up your thighs and butt, even into your "coin slot," or be located only on your labia majora. Some girls have so little it's barely noticeable; other have fluffier muffs.

Some girls find theirs easier to keep clean by trimming, shaving, or waxing. Girls might also do these things because they think sex feels better skin on skin, or that the guy prefers to go down on parts he can see well. But some guys also really like hair.

Weighty Issues

We don't have to tell you that one of the biggest ways girls feel judged is by their size. Fifteen percent of young girls have substantially disordered eating attitudes as a result, and more than five million Americans suffer from eating disorders, 90 percent of them teen girls and young women. At the same time we have unprecedented levels of obesity in America.

Studies show that it takes some people more effort to lose weight than others, thanks to genetics and environmental factors. Some girls who feel they can't meet an ideal naturally do riskier things, like live perma-diet lifestyles, constantly monitoring their food intake and sometimes bingeing hard core when they can't take the pressure.

But dieting in your teens actually makes you three times more likely to be overweight in your 20s. That's because it messes up your metabolism "set point," a weight that varies for everyone depending on natural metabolism and size. The "If only I was five pounds thinner, then he'd like me" game is one you'll never win. Weighing yourself constantly becomes addictive behavior, and your mood can fluctuate with even a one-pound move. You may get depressed after spending all week at the gym and actually gaining weight.

Getting to Know the Twins

A Diet Myth Goes Up in Smoke

Think you can puff your way to petite? A recent study finally dispelled the myth that this is possible. Teen girls who smoke cigarettes are no more likely to lose weight than girls who don't smoke.

Your feeling of connectedness to your breasts has a lot more to do with how other people treat you in response to them.

It could be a love-love situation one day, hate-hate the next, or love-hate every day. That's normal, since most of us have one breast that's slightly larger than the other anyway.

You may have caught a glimpse of other girls' naked boobs in a locker room or campus gym. But so few people have ever seen images of breasts in a nonsexualized light that they don't even know what normal is supposed to look like. Remember, boobs are built to help us reproduce and suggest to guys that we're mature enough for reproduction. Everyone's breast size, from the mammaries to the areolas, is different. Nipple color can be any shade and shape, from hard to flat to pointy to inverted. Breasts can be pert, close together, far apart, or full and low, accented by veins and hair, even a third nipple. They're all still normal.

Your Body Image and Sex

There's a huge incentive to accept, if not totally adore, your body as it is. Body-confident girls come in every shape and size, and they have a big edge on most other women because they appreciate how their physical form functions as a source of their own pleasure. That means they end up having a lot more fun in bed.

On the flip side, girls who have high levels of body discomfort and body self-consciousness have lower levels of sexual assertiveness, are less likely to use condoms, and more likely to take sexual risks and to be an extreme weight.

Body Image: What to Do

Your relationship with your body is one you have for life. You can't say that about any guy, even your friends. So you better make it a loving one, or at least friendly.

Self-Esteem from a Scalpel

You may think a tiny waist, huge rack, and high cheekbones are the paths to contentment. But before you beg your parents for a surgical quick fix, know that there isn't any evidence that it will make you happy in the long run. There are health risks with any surgery, but there's also the possibility you can get addicted to it. *The Hills'* Heidi Montag recently underwent 10 hours of cosmetic surgery, including a nose job revision, a mini–brow lift, bigger breast implants, liposuction, ear pinning, and buttock augmentation, but she says she isn't ruling out more tweaks under the knife in the future. It begs the question: How much plastic surgery is ever enough, when fake becomes norm and you don't even recognize yourself in the mirror anymore?

Also, stop trying to restyle your vagina in the way you think a guy wants it. It's up to him to adjust to you, not the other way around. Stay away from scented products and douches that can cause allergic reactions, infection, even raise your risk of contracting an STI. We'll let the fantastic folks at the *Midwest Teen Sex Show* sum it up: ". . . As for douches, would you date one? No. So don't use one."

👍 What to **SAY** to His **LIES**:

✓ "That's your opinion but it doesn't make it right. Next time keep it to yourself."
✓ "Beauty fades, dumb lasts forever."
✓ "I can always lose a few pounds, but you'll always be a jerk."
✓ "If you think I'm so awful why are you with me? I'm going to do both of us a favor and leave you so we won't have to 'tolerate' each other anymore."
✓ "Keep your ugliness to yourself. I'll make it easy for you by breaking up with you."
✓ "I'm glad that **you're** a physical model of perfection."
✓ "I think I'm beautiful and I'm going to find someone who feels the same."
✓ "The only ugly thing here is this side of your personality."
✓ "The only douche that's ever going to come near my body is you. And that was the last time."
✓ "Why would you want to be with someone you're not attracted to? I know I don't and I'm no longer into you after what you said."
✓ "I don't know how you could say something like that and claim to like me. But it makes me not like you anymore."

☞ What to **DO** if You Already Bought the **LIE:**

Surround yourself with people who think you're a rock star inside and out. If after a lot of soul-searching you're still plagued by the need to perfect a body part and really can't learn to live with it as is, we hope you will change it safely. Just preserve all the curves that make you a woman and the distinctive features that make *you* you.

Q&A

Q: It makes me self-conscious when my guy goes on and on about which celebrities are hottest and how much he wants to do them. It's not like I look anything like half of them. Why do guys talk about that stuff so much?

A: It can't be that this wishful thinking actually works, since we don't expect Jessica Biel to show up at his doorstep in this lifetime. The mass media is a strong influence on all of us, but it doesn't give us the right to rub our partner's faces in our wildest celeb fantasies. He may be oblivious to what he's doing, but if it's to actually hurt you, it pays to be a flat-out bitch in response. We like Dan Savage's advice on this one: "Don't be measured, don't wrap it up in "I" statements, no mewling about your feelings. Give him both barrels: 'If you don't knock off the asshole comments, the stupid jokes—I'm going to kick your ass out, got it?'" And don't be afraid to follow through on that promise.

Q: My mom constantly complains about how she needs to lose weight and sometimes hints that guys won't like me unless I do too. How can I get her off my back?

A: Ugh, the "You'd be so pretty if . . ." thing. Hate that. Please don't listen to her.

The mother–daughter dynamic is one of the strongest influences on how you feel about your body. Even if mom thinks you're gorgeous and vice versa, her own obsession with getting Michele Obama arms may hurt you. When you think she already looks great but she's not satisfied with anything less than perfection, you start to doubt your own looks and think you have to step it up, too. She probably isn't aware of the influence she's having on you, so you need to tell her that it makes you sad to see someone so beautiful trying to change when she doesn't have to. Don't ever feel, however, that you have to chime in with something you hate about yourself just to pick her up. That won't help either of you. If your mom doesn't knock off the subtle body bashing, acknowledge that her standards are out of whack, and just surround yourself with friends and other adult role models who think you are great just as you are.

LIE #11

"You shouldn't feel that way; you're crazy."

WHEN YOUR HEART PUTS YOUR MIND TO THE ULTIMATE TEST

🐈 Other Ways He **MIGHT** Say It

✗ "I didn't do anything wrong; you just took it too seriously."

✗ "You're way too sensitive—you must be PMSing."

✗ "I need to lie to you, because if I told the truth, you'd flip out."

✗ "You shouldn't be so insecure."

✗ "Women act too emotional."

✗ "You're acting just like your crazy family."

✗ "Female intuition is bullshit."

☞ The **TRUTH**:

Scenario: Your guy is out for the evening with his buddies. He said he'd be back by 10:00 PM and would call to say good-night. Ten o'clock comes and goes. Then the clock strikes 11:00 PM. There's still no word, so you get a little worried. Maybe something bad happened? At 11:30 PM, you text, "Hey, home okay?" No response. By midnight you're nervous, so you call him and get his voice mail. You leave a message: "Haven't heard from you; hope everything is okay."

At 12:45 AM, it's freak-out time. Where **is** he? You call again—no pickup. Another text, maybe? "Hi ya, just want to make sure ur safe—getting worried." At 2:00 AM you're officially panicked. You call his buddy to see if maybe your guy's ringer was off. "Yeah?" Your boy is the one who picks up. "Oh, my God, baby," you say. "I'm so glad to hear your voice!" "What the hell?" he says, "Why are you stalking me?" Huh? You were just checking in because you were scared. "You always do this," he goes on, "track me down and totally flip out the one time I call five minutes late." But that wasn't it at all—besides, **you** called **him** (and it wasn't five minutes). You try one more time: "I was anxious and wanted to make sure nothing happened to you, because I didn't hear from you." Then he brings in the big guns. "Oh, now it's my problem that you're paranoid? God, why do you have to act so effing crazy?" Now you **really** feel like you're losing your mind.

In stressful situations like this, it's your guy versus your gut. Before you even get a chance to fight, a boy knows that he can win in one knockout punch. Just play dirty and drop the C word (**crazy**). Questioning your sanity is the coward's way of sending you into your corner, but it works.

In fact, there's a long history of men using women's "fragile mental status" to dismiss a rightfully pissed or distressed female. In the nineteenth century, husbands even had the authority to commit their wives to mental institutions. Although getting locked up isn't the norm in relationships anymore, sensing that your guy wants control over your emotions can make you feel backed into a corner, or worse.

What to do when he labels you as either crazy or cute when you're pissy? There are at least two good reasons why you shouldn't accept this treatment from a guy. First, it's offensive. Second, passing off your feelings with the insanity stamp might be a sign in itself: your boyfriend is the one who's batshit.

The Brain Beat-Down

The more researchers learn about how the female mind processes emotion and stress, the more they understand the subtle differences between the behavior of adolescent girls and guys. Studies show that girls are a little more preoccupied with how their peers look at them. Boys, on the other hand, just want to know where they stand in the pecking order of one group. Social situations can be a lot more difficult for young women, since the mere thought of approaching other people activates the part of the brain that is associated with anxiety and depression. In fact, just sitting down at a lunch table with a group of friends can be a stressor for a girl.

Why is this happening? Crazy-making pressures for girls include needing to look right, have a boyfriend, fit in socially, and not disappoint parents and their teachers. If you can check off only one of these at a time, you might think of yourself as worthless. But just because you will be done with school, and your body and guy dramas will work themselves out eventually doesn't make it any easier to see past the temporary. Your brain actually can't fast forward that well quite yet.

Good things can come from feeling fragile or rough around the edges. What you need is an understanding of how being emotional can actually help you hone your intuition. That's one of the best weapons you have to save your ass when you're in danger—and bust a guy's when he deserves it.

"I Got a Feeling": Your Sixth Sense

Have you ever watched something go down in front of your eyes—maybe a glass breaking or a fender-bender—and thought, "Ah, I *knew* that was going to happen"? You couldn't exactly explain just how you knew, and you might not have voiced it before it took place. That doesn't mean you weren't right or that you're actually psychic. It means that you're in tune with your intuition.

You might have heard the term *women's intuition*: the idea that females have a Spidey-like sense of knowing something. Whether female intuition is actually better than guys' intuition is up for debate. What's proven is that women are better at processing nonverbal communication and other cues about how people are going to act and react. Because of subtle differences in the female brain, women may be better attuned to the environment, which helps moms not only to hear if their kid is crying but also to distinguish whether the cry is a "Gimme food!" wail versus a stinky diaper warning. Also, being smaller and having less muscular strength than guys, women are more apt to lose if they get in a battle with a man. If you're threatened by a predator, fleeing can be a better tactic than fighting back, so you're likely to be on a state of alert more often. You have to be sensitive to little cues that something isn't right, from the way a curtain is blowing to a faint smell in the air.

The funny thing is that the more women "evolve," the more the instinctive behavior that has helped them survive in a man's world gets tuned out. "Be more logical," "just look at the facts," "don't be driven by your emotions" are the sort of advice you can bet on hearing when working in a male-dominanted field. But if you spend too much time forcing yourself to be a rational little cues thinker for school and work, you tune out your ability to listen to your gut feelings. This is a problem when you rationalize away little clues as "paranoid," like your guy being more protective of his phone or seeming uninterested in what you're saying. That nagging feeling can mean something is very rotten in Denmark.

The Tech Trap:
How Your Gadgets Can Make You Crazy

For all the ways that technology helps people keep in touch with their loved ones, it also gives them a million other ways to completely screw up their relationships. Facebook a guy or send a "what's up" text too soon after a date, and you're branded a stalker. Post something on an ex's page, and the new guy may dump you for it.

Whatever issues you and a guy have with trust, they'll only be magnified when you bring technology into the picture. Same is true for respect: if he prioritizes talking on his cell phone during dinner with you or doesn't have the decency to return texts, it's a sign things aren't right. "I didn't get that message," "I didn't see your call," and "I thought I replied" are all excuses that can be used one time. However, if it's habitual, you have to ask yourself what happened to the guy who would reply within a millisecond of getting a booty text when you first met. The answer is that he's put you on his B or C list.

When It's Hard to "Just Get Over It"

SUPPOSE THAT A GUY TELLS YOU something about your appearance or judges your intelligence. He may not have meant anything by it, but to you it sounds like criticism, and it really stings. You want to brush it off and let it just wash over you. Instead your eyes fill up with tears, and you choke back a hot sensation in your throat. You hate feeling so out of control like this, but you can't help it.

When there seem to be so many reasons to flip out in a relationship, you might wonder if you really are going crazy and need help. One prime time is after a breakup. You think that because one guy doesn't want you, no one will. Or you are sure that you just need to change a little to get him back. In fact, studies show that your self-concept (the way you view yourself) changes radically after a breakup, and that you actually see yourself as a lesser person who's missing something because you don't have that partner anymore.

Situations like this, as well as stress, not getting enough sleep, or using drugs and alcohol, can be triggers for emotional problems, but being upset or angsty for a week or so doesn't mean you're clinically *anything*. However, if these feeling last longer than that, or they are so intense that you fear you might hurt yourself, it's important to talk to a healthcare professional about it, *pronto*. Once you are evaluated, you might find you were bottling up a lot of stress and pain and what you needed was a good plan of action. Or you might need consistent appointments to talk about what you're up against, and learn some problem solving skills. Getting perspective will make you feel better. Just because your heart feels broken doesn't mean that it won't ever again beat as hard or as often as it once did.

Figuring Out Your Feelings: What to Do

Understand the differences in how guys and girls deal with their feelings. Everyone has feelings; it's just that women might be more sensitive in situations that don't faze guys, like not making a team or "breaking up" with a friend. His idea of good advice for getting over it could be "Screw them, you don't need that." It might not be that helpful to you, but don't confuse a guy's misguided counsel or lack of ESP as not caring. Boys are accustomed to asking for what they want in a certain way and they might assume that girls can do the same.

When something is bothering you, speak out. Don't let anyone make you believe that you're impractical, paranoid, or crazy. Whether you're committed to someone or going solo, train yourself to listen to the little voice inside your head. It may take years to undo what you have heard as a child: "Don't be silly" or "Stop being a scaredy-cat." If you feel that things aren't right, respect that feeling, whether or not you have actual proof of its accuracy.

Finally, take care of your health, both physical and mental. Get plenty of sleep (at least eight hours a night), avoid alcohol and drugs, and find healthy ways to manage stress. Write in a journal, hit a punching bag, find a creative outlet for your feelings that doesn't involve texting or posting on Facebook.

Every day people are becoming more aware of how common mental health issues are, especially among young people. You can change the negative stigma that's attached to mental health issues by encouraging others to seek help and even by telling people you trust what you're going through. You might find that you're not as alone as you thought in feeling that way.

👍 What to **SAY** to His **LIES**:

- ✓ "This is what I feel; right or wrong, it is my feeling, and I can have it."
- ✓ "Minimizing what I'm going through doesn't make me feel better; it just makes me feel less understood by you."
- ✓ "You need to respect my opinions and feelings, not try to change them."
- ✓ "Having this feeling has nothing to do with being a girl. It's a symptom of being a smart person who doesn't automatically do what everyone tells her without thinking first."
- ✓ "You know I feel upset about this. How is telling me I'm wrong for feeling it helping?"

☞ What to **DO** if You Already Bought the **LIE:**

So if a guy is blaming your reaction to his bad behavior on PMS, you've got to call him on it. Say, "You know, I charted myself, and my period isn't due for two weeks, so nope, this isn't hormonal." Recognize that an emotionally abusive person will have a pattern of blaming others for their bad behavior or of always saying that is "inconvenient" for them to talk about it (without there ever being a good time to address it).

If you're afraid to talk openly about this stuff with your boyfriend, it may be a sign that you can't be honest and still be loved by this guy. If he can't accept you for yourself, moodiness and all, then you need to put some distance between you and the bad attitude—fast. You'll feel much better hanging out with friends who love you for who you are or being in a good relationship that doesn't come with limitations or restrictions.

Q&A

Q: I know I'm a really sensitive person, so sometimes my boyfriend will lie to me about hanging out with other girls, and he says it is to protect me from getting all worked up over nothing. Does that make sense?

A: No. "I'm only lying to you to because you force me to do it" is a cop-out. His behavior is not about protecting you at all. It's probably disguising the fact that you have a reason to be concerned about something he's done. Instead of letting you choose how to react (or learn about your choices!) he's going to save his butt first by denying you the right to decide.

In order to do this, he has to minimize what happened and blow up any tendency you have to overreact, real or imagined. That way he can sneakily rob you of the ability to judge the situation for yourself. Of course, that could cause even bigger problems. If you don't have all the information you need, letting your mind run wild could be more destructive than if he just came clean.

That brings us to the real issue here. If it was so not a big deal in the first place, why lie about it? The reason: It's probably worse than you think. He's probably getting away with more than just making you feel stupid, too. The next time you hear this line from your guy, remember what he's really trying to say: "I'm only lying to you because I think you're a freak and a fool."

Q: If I get a creepy vibe from a guy, I feel bad being unfriendly towards him without proof. How do you know when your intuition is actually wrong about a person?

A: You don't, really. If you have a bad or peculiar feeling about a stranger, don't tune it out because you can't explain it. You don't have to shout your concerns to everyone, but you don't have to go out of your way to be nice to the person, either. Trust your intuition.

LIE #12

"We should keep this between us."

THE SECRET LIVES
OF UNDERCOVER LOVERS

🐈 Other Ways He **MIGHT** Say It

✗ "We can't tell anyone about us just yet."

✗ "What we have is so good, you don't need to meet my friends and family."

✗ "It's nobody's business who I date."

✗ "We need to keep this relationship quiet."

☞ The **TRUTH**:

Few things are sexier than love on the down-low. Mix romance with a little danger, and you get an aphrodisiac that can make you think that even the blah-est of dudes is fascinating.

Clandestine hookups are so juicy that they're the fodder of everything from classics like *Romeo and Juliet* to this week's latest "Secret Love!" celebrity tabloid headline. But here's a spoiler: they never end happily, in fiction or in real life. A relationship with any guy who insists on being hush-hush about you is usually doomed, too.

The Thrill of the Secret

Most people who keep their love a secret do so at first to spare someone else's ego. Maybe you don't want your parents to know that you're sexually active, or maybe you're into a guy who's outside your circle and it would be social suicide to have it known that you're dating him. Perhaps you're in the same group of friends, or you're his ex's BFF. For whatever reason, you could decide that it's not worth broadcasting your love until you know for sure that it's going to work out.

The fake-name-in-your-cell-phone, sneak-out-and-meet-me-after-midnight-in-the-Walmart-parking-lot, don't-even-look-at-each-other-if-you're-within-a-500-foot-radius ruses can be tough to pull off. But it gives quite the rush at first. That's partly because it's one of the few things with a little mystery left to it in our overexposed, Twitter-obsessed society.

There's also a serious brain buzz that comes from hooking up when you're afraid you might get caught. When your mind processes a potentially risky situation, your body gets pumped with stress hormones. Ever hear about people in wartime falling into a torrid affair? Stressful situations actually make us more vulnerable to being snipered by Cupid.

It doesn't even matter if the threat is real, if you created it in your mind, or if you don't exactly know where the relationship is going. If you're not sure whether you two can make it to the other side in one piece, the journey seems to be much more of a thrill ride.

Why He Tells These White Lies

Even if you're not the lying type or you're not exactly sure why it has to be so hush-hush, if a guy is sexy or sweet enough, you might go along with his request for secrecy. You need to know, however, that most likely he's doing it for selfish reasons. And he probably has no intention of ever bringing you or your relationship out into the open.

Typically, a guy who is keeping mum is ashamed of you. Sorry to burst your love bubble, but there it is. We'll lay out some of the big reasons *why*, and you'll see that a few deal with factors that are out of your control, like race or religion. Even then, it might indicate that a guy isn't mature enough to deal with his insecurities or that he doesn't love you enough to stand up for you.

Race or Ethnicity

Many kids still aren't lucky enough to have family members or neighbors who understand that great relationships transcend race. If a guy fears that his relatives or his friends won't accept you, he may try to shield you from them if he thinks that they'll treat you badly. (Ditto if your parents wouldn't approve of him based on his heritage.) It's nice, in a way, to feel protected. Inevitably, though, it leaves one or both of you feeling inferior. That can start to wear on even the strongest bonds and make you question whether you have to be personally responsibly for changing minds.

Religion

Religion is another division so deep that it fuels wars all over the globe at any given moment. Again, it's usually your parents who make the biggest stink about this, since your teens and twenties are a time of spiritual exploration. You could also be dead set in your beliefs and be certain that you want to end up with someone who has the same belief system as you, then get blindsided by a guy who believes the opposite.

It's understandable if you don't identify with your parents' views but still want to respect them. You can assure your guy all you want in private that you're not in lockstep with them ideologically. What gets hard, though, is when you have to explain to him that you believe he is going to hell or is not as spiritually evolved as he should be, according to your religion. Feeling less than someone you love or being constantly judged can doom partnerships that otherwise seem to be made in heaven.

Social Status

Cliques, tribes, groups, crews—whatever you call them, they play a big role in your life right now. It's hard enough to maintain friendships when you're dating someone. If you're not in the same circle, it can be agony, especially if one person looks down on the other.

Sometimes this has more to do with how much money your family has or what part of town you live in. You may feel as if you have to prove yourself when you're around his friends to fit in, or vice versa. But what really hurts? The fact that this guy won't defend you to his friends or prune them from his life altogether.

Family Ties

We inherit more than just the color of our parents' eyes—sometimes we get their beefs, too. Whether your family's reputation in town is justified or undeserved, it can come back to bite you. A lot of adults look at kids as an extension of themselves, so if your parents didn't grow up there or go to the "right" school, you could feel like an outsider. There's also the possibility that you'll be followed by a rumor about a sibling and have the same image applied to you. It's uncool and unfair, but it's not uncommon in smaller communities—at least in those packed with small minds.

Still, there are some valid reasons that a guy might want to keep you from his family. For instance, if they have troubles with money, abuse, or drugs and alcohol, he might be ashamed and worried that you'll condemn them. It's also possible that he brought a girl home in the past and his parents blew their relationship way out of proportion. He's worried that they'll start calling you their daughter before he's ready for date number three, so he won't introduce you to mom and pop if he's still making up his mind. This is especially true if they don't live in the same town. Either way, it's a sign that things are way more complicated and twisted than you realize.

Looks

Sorry to say this, but some guys feel entitled to supermodel-caliber arm candy—this, despite the fact that they themselves have been thrashed twenty times till Tuesday with an ugly stick. Shitty, we know. If a Marisa Miller look-alike isn't available, he might "settle" for a perfectly pretty, normal girl, but only behind closed doors. If you're sweet and supportive—and, more important, will put out—he'll happily indulge that in private. He might even tell you you're hot. But because he's too wrapped up in appearances and doesn't want to be teased by his friends, he'll give you all the courtesy of a leper in public. This doesn't feel good because it *isn't* good.

Age

From age 14 on, most girls tend to date boys who are one to three years older than they are. That's understandable, since guys are a good 18 months behind girls in the puberty race until the end of adolescence. A dude with a couple of extra years under his belt can validate your coolness and maturity like nothing else can. Finally, someone who makes you feel ahead of your time is a good thing!

What about the ones who are a good deal older—four, six, even ten years older? The ones who are attractive like hot vampires in the movies. (And sometimes he's afraid of being seen in daylight with you.) Your connection with him feels otherworldly, indescribable even. All you know is that only he has the power to see your brilliance among all the beige followers at school.

Face it: most guys aren't worried about looking like a cradle-robbing sleaze; in fact, there are bragging rights for guys who are able to claim that a hot young thing is theirs. So if you're being forced to keep it quiet by your older boyfriend, most likely it's because there's something seriously wrong with the situation. For example, his fossil fetish would disturb your parents or he's in a position of influence, such as your teacher, a coach, or a religious leader. The vast majority of older men you come in contact with at school, work, or religious services know that young girls look up to them and get crushes on them from time to time. They also know that there is a moral and even legal line that can't be crossed. They have too much power over you and your future to risk abusing it by getting involved.

If a man does toe over the boundary, you need to know that he's taking advantage of your youth as well as the fact that your impulse control isn't totally developed. This means that you might do things that an older woman would know better than to try because it would hurt her, such as having unprotected sex. (FYI: You're more likely to get pregnant if your partner is six or more years older than you!) It may seem unfair to have age dictate your love, but there's a reason that laws are in place that make sex with adults illegal: it's to protect minors.

Being in the Same Workplace

To have a kick-ass career one day, you'll probably have to spend a lot of time doing internships and taking on work-study or part-time jobs. And if this requires you to be alongside dudes, the chances are that you might fall for one of them. (Forty percent of Americans end up dating someone in the workplace.) It's okay to not want to involve your boss and coworkers in your romantic drama if it's going to be a fleeting thing, such as just a summer job or a one-month internship. Then it's actually smart to spend a few weeks quietly sorting out if you two really click before putting it in the company newsletter (as well as checking with HR to see what the company rules are!).

If things are still going well a month or two into it, you need to let your boss know. He or she probably suspects something, anyway. In close quarters, people can smell a lot more than coffee brewing. Of course, this means understanding the rules about employee relationships on the job. In most cases, boss-subordinate relationships are prohibited, but at times even people on the same level aren't allowed to date. You need to carefully weigh whether it's worth putting your job in jeopardy. Isn't it enough that he has too much power over you emotionally? You have to give him power over your job, too?

Why Undercover Love Rarely Works

When you're each feeding off only the other person, it's like being plugged into one power source with no other outlet to draw from: the circuits blow fast. When researchers looked at people who were in open unions or top-secret ones, those who had to hide their relationships rated them as lower quality from the very start. Then, only a few weeks into them, they found that the factors that initially made the fling a thrill faded fast and even turned into huge problems.

One of the biggies is keeping the fact that you're giddy in lust with someone from the people you love. Try as you might to keep your chipper mood in check, you're wired to operate on one principle: When you're happy and you know it, flap your lips. So what happens when your BFF asks, "Why are you so smiley all of a sudden?" Keep in mind that this girl knows everything about you, inside and out. Answering, "Uh, I just had a really delicious, um, bean burrito" probably won't cut it.

Also, it's a hell of a lot of work to keep your bond with someone a secret, especially if you still live under your parents' roof. What happens if you have no place to go to be together, to be alone? Are late-night chats under the covers really enough to sustain the relationship? Technology makes it harder to hide from electronic snoops. Picture your little brother getting hold of your phone and listening to your voice mail. Your guy's ex could also hack into his e-mail or Facebook account and forward steamy messages to everyone in his address book and on his friend list. Hell, someone in Bangladesh can spot two lovebirds in Boston holding hands by checking out Google Earth. And you still have to worry about old-school busting, such as your mom coming across a note in your jeans pocket. It won't take long to come to this conclusion: If you have to keep your relationship a secret, you shouldn't be in it.

Being in a Secret Relationship

Know that a good guy will honor your relationship. That means everything from being on time for dates to being open about actually *dating* you. Here's what he won't do: tell you to lie; pressure you into any sexual activity; convince you to stop hanging out with friends and family; or care too much about what his own crew thinks to undermine someone he loves.

There are times that it's simply not safe to be aboveboard with a new love. But most of the time, secret relationships force you to lie to people who care about you, and it cuts you off from your support system. When you're not getting input from family and friends, it's harder to see what's acceptable and what's sucky behavior on his part. If you're hiding the relationship for one of the following reasons, it's a clear sign that you shouldn't be with him and you need to leave the relationship:

- You could lose your job or opportunity for education if someone found out.
- One of you could be punished under the law because of an age difference.
- You're enabling bad habits in each other, like lying, abusing substances, cheating on a partner, or having risky sex.

These don't apply to you? Fine. But even if you think you can pull off a secret relationship, ask yourself if you know the real reason it's so necessary. On his end, it's usually to control you or to deal with his shame about being with you. Do a gut check on what he says in private and does in public. A boy shouldn't be telling you anything he wouldn't say out loud walking through the mall. So if he can't admit to liking you within earshot of friends or family, it means that he's not sure about you and that you're not worth all the love, attention, and affection that he could give a girl he's really into.

👍 What to **SAY** to His **LIES**:

✓ "Forcing me to keep a secret is the same as lying."

✓ "If you don't think that I'm the same great person in public that I am when we're alone, then I can't keep seeing you in private."

✓ "It feels like we're living a lie, and that doesn't feel right to me."

✓ "Why can't you be honest about the fact that we're dating? It makes me think that you don't really want to be with me."

✓ "You're being dishonest, and I'm helping you to do that. I don't want to live my life that way, so I can't take part anymore."

✓ "I believe that you love me but you also must show me by being public about it."

✓ "You say one thing but do another. Since you refuse to back up your promises, you've forced me to take action."

✓ "I might think that you're right for me, but this situation we're in isn't. It doesn't seem like it's changing, so I have to end things between us."

✓ "I always pictured myself being with a guy who gives me his time and his love. You can't do that now."

☞ What to **DO** if You Already Bought the **LIE**:

If you're been taken for granted or made to feel invisible by a guy, know that he will keep this going only as long as you let him. It's totally within your rights to be "difficult" about this, meaning not easily suckered. Give him an ultimatum that's contingent on something he really can do. (That is, you can't say, "Change religions just so you won't get a dirty look from my grandpa at the next holiday dinner." However, telling his friends about your relationship tomorrow is doable.) Claiming he can't do it is a coward's move.

This is especially true if you're involved with a guy who's already attached to someone else. If he says that he wants to leave but that he doesn't know how or the timing isn't right, he is wrapping a Snuggie around this truth: "Do not expect to me leave my girlfriend for you, because it's not going to happen." It's lazy and unattractive, but it's comfortable (at least for him). It's also your cue to move on. You don't have to beat yourself up about it, just examine whether you intentionally go for guys who are out of reach.

In the future, put yourself in situations where you'll attract the right kind of guys. This means focusing on school, work, and hobbies that will keep you too busy to waste time sneaking around. When you're out doing stuff that is genuinely good for your brain and body, you free yourself to find someone who would be proud to skywrite his love for you.

Q&A

Q: I'm a private person. Isn't that a good enough reason to let me keep my relationship to myself?

A: Sure, it's a natural response to our TMI culture. Some things, like details about the little tongue swirl he does that makes your toes curl, should be sacred. But there's a difference between *private* and *secret*. The people in the best relationships may be private about how they really interact behind closed doors, but they aren't secretive about showing their love. You *do* have to be able to answer honestly whether you are actually dating someone if you've been going out for months and already dropped the L-bomb.

Q: I'm dating a guy who's in a different social circle, and we both agreed that it would be better to keep it secret. He's great to me when we're alone, but I get pissed off when we're at school and he flirts with other girls. I know it's just so that people will think he's single, and he's not really seeing them. But is it bad that it makes me feel awful?

A: No, it should. He's toying with your emotions. How can you be sure he's not going after these girls, too? If he can do it with one, he can do it with many. Our advice: Get over yourselves and come clean.

LIE #13

"Don't worry,
I won't show
anyone these
pictures."

LOVE AND SEXT IN THE DIGITAL AGE

🐈 Other Ways He **MIGHT** Say It

✗ "The video camera isn't really on."

✗ "It's fun, don't be so uptight. Trust me."

✗ "Let me tape this now—we can erase it later."

✗ "It'll be better if we can watch it on screen."

✗ "Picture-mail me a shot of what you're wearing."

✗ "It's artistic, not dirty or porn."

☞ The **TRUTH**:

The word sexting has become so common that if you hear it one more freaking time, someone is going down. Maybe the idea of it has been blown out of proportion in the media; nevertheless, the consequences haven't.

One of the largest and most recent studies on sexting (done by the Associated Press and MTV) brought its scope into sharp focus. More than one-quarter of teens had engaged in sexting, which is defined as sharing sexually explicit photos, videos, and chat by cell phone or online. Ten percent had sent out nude shots of themselves, but as you can imagine, it's not the guys who are doing most of the revealing. About half of high school guys had seen a nude shot of a female classmate, according to another study. And 17 percent of those who had a received a sext message passed it on to someone else, usually more than one person.

What the numbers don't say is exactly how a racy photo, video, or audiotape of you can go viral, like a bad STI. At least some infections can be cured. A black mark on your digital record, however, is forever, and it can be seen by millions of people. You have absolutely no control over it the moment you hit "send." All you have is the promise of being haunted by the Ghost of Penis Past for years to come.

"You're a Natural":
Why Flesh in a Flash Might Feel Right

Part of you knows that broadcasting photos or videos of your-self doing anything racier than hanging out at a family barbecue or a school function is a bad idea. But when a guy asks to see some of your body parts, the responsible half of you says, "Sayonara, lady!" The girl who takes over is one who wants to be the chilled-out, open-minded, easygoing, wild child. And come to think of it, you *do* look super cute in your red boy shorts and no top. Besides, your guy is pouting and saying "pretty please." So what are you going to do, listen to reason or listen to him? Even Beyoncé seems to have his back: "You want me naked? If you liking this position, you can tape it on your video phone."

A lot of girls today know that there's power in being seen as sexy, and of course it's flattering to hear a guy say you have a sick body. "Show me that ass, babe," he says. "I can't wait for you to see how fine you are." What if maybe, just maybe, someone saw how hot you are and thought you should be famous or a model? Then you could go from nobody to notorious overnight. (One study from 2005 found that 31 percent of American teenagers expect to be famous. Not just *hope* or *wish*—they think it's *inevitable!*)

One of the biggest reasons you might consider sending some-thing explicit is to please a guy. Sometimes it feels liberating to expose yourself to someone emotionally, so why not do it physi-cally? Maybe, you think, it will convince him to be into you a little more.

Doing this to try to lure someone you like into liking you back is bad news from the start. For one thing, you don't even have the basic level of trust and communication to ask him point-blank if he likes you. Why is it a good idea to give him access to your body before you know if he even wants it? Furthermore, what if he thinks it's uncool that you disrespected yourself this way? He could laugh at you or spread it around out of disgust. Oh, and he still might pass it on even if he is into you, to prove just how many hot girls are after him.

"But I Trust Him!": How Your Boyfriend Can Screw You Forever (Not in a Good Way)

Worst of all is when you engage in sexting or send a racy video to prove a commitment to a guy. Remember when actress Vanessa Hudgens's nude photos were leaked? Her own boyfriend did that!

You may think that you have less to lose than the *High School Musical* star, but you can't assume that you are immune to the pressure. One recent survey showed that 60 percent of teens had been pressured to let someone take nude photos of them at least once. Your guy may play the sentimental card, saying that he just wants the photos to remind him of you when you aren't there. You don't want him looking at some other girl instead, do you? The threat of losing him to someone else can be all it takes to wear a smart girl down.

What happens the next time you have an argument and he gets vindictive? Now he has blackmail material literally at his finger-tips. If he can't control himself when he sees you looking at another guy or when you threaten to break up with him, all he has to do is make one click, and those photos are in your dad's in-box.

Former Miss California USA Carrie Prejean learned this the hard way. Her first boyfriend betrayed her by exposing topless and nude shots plus a fetish video she allegedly took herself for him at age 19. "It was the biggest mistake of my life," she said in the aftermath. "I was sending a boyfriend at the time who I loved and cared about, you know, a video of me. I was a teenager at the time. Never did I think it would ever come out. . . . It was bad judgment." If you think that's mortifying, consider this: Reports say that her mom was in the room when the lawyers from the Miss California USA pageant pressed play! "I've learned a lot about people and just what they'll do to make some extra money," Prejean said to the media, adding, "Be careful. Nothing is private anymore."

How Far and Fast It Can Go

People with exhibitionist streaks have always run the risk of getting overexposed in public. Today, though, you don't have to get off on putting yourself out there to get burned. Practically everyone has a camera phone or video capability in his or her pocket. Other people might be snapping off shots of you without your knowledge—not just simple photos, but also videos and webcams.

Just how thin is the line between one person and the entire world? Check out these very possible ways that an image of you can go viral at the hands of one guy:

- Accidentally cc'ing an entire address book
- Sitting on a phone (a.k.a. "ass-dialing") or letting it bounce around in a bag so that the wrong buttons get pushed
- Leaving a phone or other electronic device unattended at a party where someone else finds it
- Playing a video for an entire frat house or in the locker room after a sports team practice

- Posting a picture on Facebook after the two of you have had a fight
- Passing an image on to an ex who still holds a grudge
- Showing a photo or a video to another guy to "pay him" for letting him see shots of his girlfriend
- Taking his media card to a photo store or a drugstore and forgetting to erase the photos
- Having his laptop stolen or borrowed by someone who finds the shots and spreads them around
- Letting his future girlfriend see a shot of you to prove that she has nothing to worry about (you're not as hot as she is), and then she spreads it around because she's jealous
- Having an ex-friend sell you out when you get in an argument. (Remember back when Paris Hilton and Nicole Richie were besties? Nicole allegedly played a video of what she claimed was Paris hosting *Saturday Night Live* at a party. It turned out to be Hilton's infamous sex tape instead. Paris's response: "Not hot"—she effectively ended their friendship.)

Regardless of how photos go viral and out of control, the consequences are the same, and you'll have to face them again and again. Here are some of the biggies:

- Having to sit down in a pew, on a bus, in a cubicle, or in a salon chair knowing that the people to your left, to your right, in front of you, and behind you may have seen your private parts
- Explaining to admissions officers, summer internship coordinators, pageant directors, teachers, coaches, camp

directors, potential employers, future boyfriends, and even in-laws why you thought it was a good idea to expose so much skin to the whole damn world

- Feeling ashamed or stupid when your parents ask, "Honestly, what did you think would happen?" or worse yet, defending the decision to your little sister or your future kids' horny teenage friends (ugh!)
- Wondering whether guys really like you for you or if they're just curious about the body they saw buck-naked
- Walking down the halls of your school knowing that all eyes are on you and that even kids at the neighboring schools have seen images of you overexposed
- Being suspended from school, getting kicked off a team or out of a club that is important to you, or losing a leadership position in an extracurricular activity

If you think you can handle all of this now, know that you could be limiting your opportunities in the future, even banishing yourself altogether from certain careers, such as politics or the military. A perfect example: Carmen Kontur-Gronquist, former mayor of Arlington, Oregon, was ousted from office because of a MySpace photo of her in her underwear that was taken well before she ever decided to run for office.

Today, many employers will Google job applicants to find additional information about them. If something is on the Internet, posted by you or someone else, it's viewable even after the website it first went on is taken down. (You can cache pages forever on an internal site, and anyone can save a screen shot as a different file type on a hard drive.)

Revealing Photos: What to Do

That one shot of you can be fatal to your future. That goes for your reputation now, your relationships in the future, and even your career 20 years from today.

Every time you take a photo or do something in public where someone could see it, ask yourself if it would pass the "fridge test." That is, would you put it on your refrigerator at your parents' house? If your grandpa saw this, would he be proud? How about if this photo popped up in a slide show at your wedding?

Be careful, too, every time you're in a shot with someone else that could be misinterpreted later (e.g., you and your best friend are laughing and hugging, but it might be taken as "lesbian foreplay" on a porn site). Always think, "If a potential employer saw it, could it damage my chances of getting the job or internship I want?" Blowing kisses or hugging your boyfriend is fine, but too much panty in that picture, being topless, or even a Miley Cyrus–style back-only pose is a no-no. More skin equals more potential for scandal.

If a guy is pressuring you to do something digitally that you don't want to do, it's abusive. Make it very clear that you being his girlfriend does not give him the right to document you for his camera for any reason, sexual or otherwise. This takes a face-to-face sit-down at a table, not just a spat in which you voice your opinions in anger.

Don't ever pass along a nude or seminude photo you receive of anyone, whether it's a boyfriend or an enemy. At least two teens committed suicide as a result of the harassment and bullying they experienced after a sext message they sent to a guy got out. Could you live with something like that on your head if you casually forwarded a shot of someone to another person? If not, just delete it and forget it.

👍 What to **SAY** to His **LIES**:

- ✓ "I'm a lot better in person. You'll have to take my word for it."
- ✓ "I don't want to be a porn star. I have bigger goals than that."
- ✓ "If people saw it, they could get the wrong idea about me."
- ✓ "This scares me. I'm not doing it."
- ✓ "I know you'd never spread this, but I can't trust that someone else won't come across it and do that."

👉 What to **DO** if You Already Bought the **LIE**:

Short of hopping into a time machine and getting a redo on the day you made the mistake, there isn't much you can do except hold your head high and start repairing your reputation. You should formulate a decent explanation of why it happened and how you'll prevent it in the future, so that you're prepared to discuss it with employers and admissions counselors. "I made a mistake and I'm not proud of it, but here's what I learned from it" is a good start.

Q&A

Q: My boyfriend is begging me to give him a topless shot of myself for his birthday. Is it okay to do it if it's a gift?

A: A cake from a naughty bakery is about the only the form of boobage you should be bestowing on this birthday boy. It doesn't matter if he gave you a photo first, either. Just as you'd send off a bracelet an ex gave you to www.cashforgold.com, a guy can treat your picture as a moneymaker, too. You won't see a pretty penny from it, but you may see yourself on some creepy amateur porn site dedicated to exes getting revenge on their former loves.

Q: Most celebrities' careers are actually helped by sex tapes. If actresses don't get in trouble, why would I?

A: That depends on your definition of career. Britney Spears, Kim Kardashian, Paris Hilton, Pamela Anderson, and Kendra Wilkinson each had a sex tape, but it's not like they're out winning Oscars. It can actually stop you before you become a success. Online posts of sexy photos of *American Idol* contestant Antonella Barba didn't get her kicked off the show, but it did stop Americans from voting for her. That blow was harsher than any nasty quip Simon could ever spew.

You have to think about how a tape could jeopardize your future, not to mention what it would be like to have your creepy balding supervisor, the one with the hideous coffee breath, viewing it. Contrary to Hollywood wisdom, there are other ways to earn a dollar and respect than flashing your boobs.

LIE #14

"Have a drink or some weed; it'll make you feel better."

SEX, DRUGS, AND THE ROCKY ROLES THEY PLAY TOGETHER

🐕 Other Ways He **MIGHT** Say It

✗ "Sex feels better after you have a beer or a smoke."

✗ "Getting high will bring us closer."

✗ "You need to relax more; this will help."

☞ The **TRUTH**:

Alcohol and marijuana use among teens is now on the rise after a decade-long decline. However, girls aren't doing it just to fit in with friends or have fun at parties. Experts say that girls are relying more on drugs and alcohol to get close to a guy and then to cope after a breakup. Comparatively more guys use these substances, but for some reason these substances are harder habits to kick for women than for men.

If a guy tells you that a little booze or weed will help you loosen up during a hookup or bond you together, you need to question whether he's drunk or high. No one in his right mind would think that this is a good idea for a truly healthy sexual or romantic connection to someone.

Your Brain on Drugs

Your brain is still developing into your late 20s, so even if drinking and smoking are rites of passage for many in middle school, this doesn't change the fact that your mind isn't ready for them. In fact, you need only half the amount of booze to cause the same damage in comparison to adult brains. And marijuana use is three times more likely to lead to a dependence among adolescents than among adults.

Both marijuana and alcohol have negative effects on the brain, but they do it in different ways. Booze shrinks the brain, whereas marijuana expands it, and that's not a good thing when it affects your ability to learn and process information. You think classes are hard now? The poor cognitive function that comes with pot use can make enough of an impact to lower your grades by at least one level, and that can last up to a month after you smoke.

Drugs and alcohol affect not only your ability to think but also your capacity to feel. Pot in particular hurts more than your ability to study, because it actually changes the way your brain processes emotions and other people's social cues. The part of your brain that acts as your emotional control-center—think of it as the tough-love friend who keeps you in check when you need someone to tell it to you straight—is completely out to lunch. That makes you less likely to be able to decipher what the cryptic text from your crush *really* means or to control your anger when you think that a friend is stabbing you in the back.

Because of the differences between male and female brains, women may be more prone to become chronic drinkers. They actually become dependent more quickly than guys do. In addition, alcohol causes more damage and does it faster to the parts of the brain that help us to remember, plan, and process information.

Why Experimenting Can Wait

WHAT WOULD IT BE LIKE TO WAKE UP one day and realize that the best years of your life have disappeared? That's what can happen if you start using any substance before your brain is fully developed. And the earlier you begin, the worse the long-term damage can be.

How Booze and Drugs Wreck Your Body

Teens who drink also have more disruptions in their menstrual cycles and suffer unplanned pregnancies, possibly because they don't know when their periods are coming and are thus more likely to have sex at the wrong time.

Both booze and drugs screw up your sleep; they not only make it harder to feel rested, they also mess up the processes that take place when you're snoozing. You need sleep so your body can release hormones that help you mature physically and mentally. Also, regular heavy drinking increases your risk of liver disease.

If all that doesn't make an impact, here's one thing that might: Have you ever seen party girls in Hollywood when they're not caked in makeup for the red carpet? They end up having a face like a catcher's mitt before they're 25. They might have the cash to get plastic surgery every year to fix it, but you don't. And getting a liver transplant ain't easy.

Having Sex Under the Influence

Does it really feel better to get it on when you're high? Studies show that a minimal amount of alcohol and marijuana may lead some people to rank sex as more satisfying. But, in fact, the more you smoke and drink, the less interest you'll actually have in sex. You'll have less lubrication and a dry mouth if you've been drinking a lot, and neither one makes sex much fun.

In spite of how intoxication can make hooking up less fun, teens who use drugs and/or alcohol are five times more likely to have sex than teens who do not use these substances. Some girls who use drugs or alcohol as part of their foreplay do it because they're ashamed of feeling sexual, or they feel the need for a mental release to unleash their inner vixen.

But the opposite can be true for guys. A boy could use your sloppiness as a way to get away with lying. How? Easy: when you're drunk, it's much more difficult for you to pick up on little cues that he's not telling the whole truth, because alcohol impairs your judgment. For example, if you're only a little buzzed, your brain still might let you ask the right questions ("Do you have a girlfriend?" or "You put on a condom, right?"), which makes you think that you're still in control. But that safeguard instinct might not stick around to fully hear or understand the answers. Since you can't focus on multiple details at once, you might not notice his buddies snickering in the background when he says, "Nah, I'm single."

The glowy peak of a high could you make you think that you're more into him than you normally would be (hi ya, beer goggles!). If a few drinks are all it takes for you to buy his lines, he will think that booze equals mission accomplished. In fact, a guy may be really invested in keeping you liquored up because you let a lot of things slide when you're not sober.

Even if you promise yourself that you will only go to a certain point or you're vigilant about protection, you can't trust your brain to take good care of your body if it's under the influence. The use of drugs and alcohol has been associated with risky sex time after time in studies. An incurable infection can be the buzz kill of your lifetime. And you'll know that the party's over when you have a kicking bundle of joy in your belly for nine months that will take up all your free time for the next 18 years.

> **Words to Love By**
> "Cold sober, I find myself absolutely fascinating."
> —Katharine Hepburn

The Scary Side of Imbibing

It could start out innocently. You hear, "Just come hang out in my room, we'll just chill," and so you go somewhere with a guy you aren't really sure about. Perhaps you might not pick up on the cue that a guy thinks you're trying to seduce him when you think you're just being friendly. You won't be able to notice that a guy is trying to get you into an isolated area or that he's telling you to drink more, refilling your cup with God-knows-what substance. Once you're too trashed, you can't resist as well physically or make your intentions to not have sex known as clearly. (In one study of date rapists, at least three quarters of them said that they had gotten women drunk in order to increase their chances of getting sex from them.)

A really frightening study showed that 40 percent of guys thought it was okay to force sex on a date who was drunk. When you're drinking alcohol, it's easier for him to slip you a date rape drug (a "roofie"). It incapacitates you so you can't resist physically and won't remember anything afterwards.

Picking Up a Sad Habit

SOME GIRLS WHO SMOKE OR DRINK to get to know a guy or to feel close him find that the habit lingers long after the love affair is over. As a relationship souvenir, a mind-altering substance can be a lot more comforting than some cheesy teddy bear that the guy got you for Valentine's Day; however, it can also be a bad habit that will stay with you long after you've kicked his ass to the curb.

The consequences for girls are a lot more severe than just a hangover. Girls are more prone to anxiety and depression, and alcohol actually contributes to depression. Moreover, marijuana is anxiogenic, which means that it causes anxiety. You could end up creating a serious mental issue for yourself, one that you might not have had in the first place if you'd just found another way to deal with a short-lived period of sadness or anxiety.

Nervous Wrecks

YOU KNOW THAT YOU SHOULD NEVER drive when you've been drinking or doing any mind-altering drugs, but it's hard to say *no* to the guy you trust or to an older dude who seems to have it together. You might not want to offend him, and he has promised you that he can handle it. "Guys have a bigger tolerance than girls," he says, putting the keys into the ignition.

Do not believe this under any circumstances—you are putting your life at risk. Automobile accidents are the number one cause of death among kids ages 15 to 19; among guys between 15 and 20 who were involved in fatal crashes, more than a quarter had been drinking.

Even when sober, teens are less likely to recognize dangerous situations and are more prone to speed and underestimate how hazardous a situation can be. Don't think that pot isn't as bad; driving under the influence of marijuana almost doubles the risk of a fatal road crash. It's hard to picture what it would be like to be killed, but think about something you *can* imagine, like being confined to a wheelchair or a hospital bed for the rest of your life. If you don't want to find out what that's like, don't ever get in a car with someone who has been drinking or doing mind-altering drugs (legal or illegal).

Getting High: What to Do

Stop using now. It doesn't make you funny, creative, original, fun, or sexy. It just makes you *think* you are.

It can be hard to abstain when the perception is that you're bitchy or boring for not doing what everyone else does. Please trust us when we say that most guys think that the statement "OMG, I was so wasted last night!" is about as attractive as saying "Does this make me look fat?" or "I plead guilty, your honor."

The kind of guy you want to be with will hate it when a girl gets sloppy. In fact, if your goal is marriage, studies show that the likelihood of getting hitched is much lower for teen girls who abuse alcohol and drugs, even as they approach their late 20s. Regardless of whether you want your Mrs. degree or your Ph.D. in singlehood, you'd be smart not to put obstacles like drugs and alcohol in your way.

For the rest of your life, *never* get into a car with a driver who has been drinking or doing mind-altering drugs. Take the keys, if you can, but more important, take yourself out of the situation, even if it means waking up your parents at 3:00 AM or spending $100 on a cab. It beats ending up as a tragic statistic in a newspaper article about another promising life lost. You were destined to create a greater legacy than that.

👍 What to **SAY** to His **LIES**:

✓ "Why is it so important to you that I have some of it? I'm fine as I am."

✓ "I'd rather remember our time together than draw a huge blank later."

✓ "Actually, I read that it does some really bad stuff to the brain at our age. I'm not going to risk getting dumber or sadder, even just one time."

✓ "I don't need that to feel good."

✓ "I don't care if it's a natural drug. It makes me feel like I'm not myself. Besides, why would I want anything that makes me more paranoid and hungry than I already am?"

☞ What to **DO** if You Already Bought the **LIE:**

If you find yourself imbibing too much of any substance, the first thing you need to do is remove yourself from the situation. Say, "I'm not feeling up to it" and get in touch with a trusted person (not the guy you just met at the party) who can get you out of there immediately. While you wait, drink plenty of water and eat starchy food to help lessen the effects.

If you're using to feel less anxious or sad, perhaps after breaking up with a guy or because you're solo, it's especially important that you seek help for this from a pro. No one should have to go through a painful time alone. You need someone to convince you that you're capable of more than this. Talk to a counselor who can show you that you have the power to get better, and you can do it without a guy or a substance. It can be tough to admit that you're using drugs or alcohol. The truth is that a health-care professional will be really happy that you came clean so that he or she can figure out how to help you.

Q&A

Q: My boyfriend keeps telling me that pot is no big deal because it's natural, you know, "just weed."

A: Weed is not as "natural" as you think. Many growers use pesticides and other chemicals that certainly aren't organic to grow it.

As for the medical excuse, if you're not seriously ill, marijuana is not for you. Think about it this way: You wouldn't do chemotherapy or AZT if you didn't have cancer or AIDS. And *smoking* pot could actually increase your likelihood of getting lung cancer (pot smoke has been linked to lung carcinomas).

Q: My guy is pretty addicted to alcohol and sometimes takes Oxycontin. I don't want to be around him when he does it, but he is such a sweet guy when he's not using, and I want to help him through his addiction. How much longer should I stick with it?

A: Not another day. Sorry, but he's never going to change as long as the good things in his life—namely, you—stay exactly the same. Until he loses you as a consequence, he'll have no incentive to quit.

That said, you need to know that it's not your responsibility to fix him up. Accept that you can't change him; you can only encourage him to get help. You can even find places for him to go or support groups but most importantly get to a "friends and family of" (Alanon) meeting yourself ASAP.

LIE #15

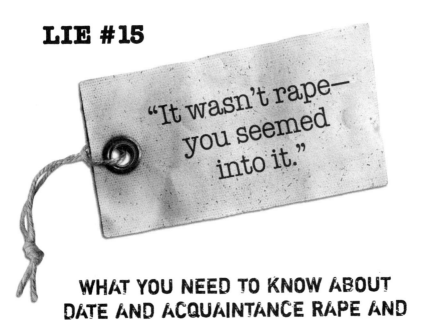

"It wasn't rape—you seemed into it."

WHAT YOU NEED TO KNOW ABOUT DATE AND ACQUAINTANCE RAPE AND OTHER FORMS OF SEXUAL ASSAULT

🐾 Other Ways He **MIGHT** Say It

✗ "Relax, it was just sex."

✗ "The way you were dressed and acting, you were practically begging for it."

✗ "**No** really means **yes**."

✗ "All women want to be dominated."

✗ "If you didn't want to have sex, you shouldn't have come over to my place."

✗ "You said yes; you just don't remember because you were drunk."

☞ The **TRUTH**:

As you're exploring what feels right to you sexually, you might find yourself in situations where a guy tries to push you further than what feels comfortable. The catch is that, even if you say **no**, there are some guys who won't respect that. Unfortunately, sexual violence is sadly common for girls your age. One in three teenage girls experiences an act of sexual violence before age 18.

Sexual violence can come in different forms, but all of them can have effects that go way beyond the physical. Some guys will try to make you think that something that is actually rape is just sex that you regret or secretly wanted. Even other girls are guilty of minimizing rape experiences and blaming them on the victim.

That's why it's important for you to understand exactly what qualifies as sexual violence, and why guys use stereotypes about women's sexuality to excuse it. The more you know, the better you can defend yourself against victimization of the mind and the spirit.

Sexual Assault Versus Rape

The terminology for different forms of sexual violence might be confusing, but the experiences have one thing in common: they involve someone doing something you don't want. *Sexual assault* is usually defined as any unwanted sexual contact, such as touching, kissing, fondling, or groping sexual body parts. Even if you don't express the fact that you don't like it, it still counts as an assault. It doesn't have to be paired with violence, like a slap of the face or a hand over your mouth.

Anytime a guy forces you to do something sexually with violence or threats, or when you're in fear of him hurting your body, this is assault—but it might also be rape. In most states, rape involves the use of force or the threat of force to have vaginal or anal intercourse, oral sex, rough sexual activity that is nonconsensual, or unprotected sex. Penetration with either a body part or an object qualifies.

There doesn't have to be a gun or a knife involved for the coercion to count as rape. In fact, nearly 80 percent of rapes involve no weapon. And it doesn't matter if you're bigger than a guy or don't fight back physically. The issue is consent: if you didn't give it or were not able to, then the act is rape.

You might be surprised to find out that not so long ago, most people connected rape with a stranger jumping out of the bushes and attacking. It's actually the least likely form of rape to happen to you. Surveys show that 93 percent of young people who are sexually assaulted know the attacker. The most common kind of rape is acquaintance rape or date rape. These two terms are often used interchangeably—both mean forced sexual activity with someone you know or maybe even consented to go out with. This might be a guy from the neighborhood or a friend of a friend.

It doesn't matter if you've been together one week or two years; it is possible to be raped when you're on a date, or even if you are a girlfriend or wife. Studies show that women who have been victimized by their partners are more likely to be raped multiple times, unlike women who are raped by acquaintances or strangers. It can make the effect even more severe and traumatizing than you can possibly imagine.

Sexual Harassment 101

WHETHER IT'S A CATCALL or a slap on the butt, you know how frustrating unwanted sexual attention is. You might not know, however, that most of it happens where you're supposed to feel safe: at school.

Approximately 79 percent of sexual harassment among peers takes place at school, usually in the form of jokes, grabbing body parts like the butt or the breasts, or commenting on someone's physical appearance. There are laws that protect you from this type of discrimination on school property. If the school doesn't follow through on a report of harassment, it can be sued or lose federal funding, and you could be awarded damages.

Why Guys Push the Limits

It's hard for boys to understand what it's like for a girl to walk every day among people who could overpower her at any time. The physical difference is only part of it. A guy might say things like "You're a tease, you owe me this" or "That's not fair, you can't just work me up like that and walk out of here." Their feelings of entitlement and their ability to make you feel guilty is a bad combination.

This puts women in the uncomfortable position of being the gatekeeper. Believing that you're the one who is responsible for holding a guy back from getting what he wants is a big burden. Even though most people understand that sex is never a given, it's hard for some girls to say *no* when they think they owe a guy something just because he bought them dinner, for instance.

Some women find it easier to just have sex than to explain that they're not into it or that they'd rather go to sleep. And it's a lot better, they think, than seeming "ungrateful" or risking that he'll get mean. Of course, this is a form of force in itself.

If you do resist a guy's advances, that still doesn't mean that he won't interpret the red light as a green one. Many boys are brought up to think that chasing and pressuring girls is what a "real man" is supposed to do. They hear it all the time in messages like "Nothing easy is worth having," and "Never take no for an answer."

This culture of male entitlement may explain why, in one study, up to 16 percent of men said that they would commit rape if they thought they could get away with it. There's another factor playing into this atmosphere called the *rape myth*. That's the perception that women want to be forced into sexually violent situations because it turns them on. It doesn't refer to rough consensual sex, which can be pleasurable for some women. It means being forced to do something sexual against your will. Studies show that simply believing that it's okay to use sexual violence against a woman because she'll secretly enjoy it makes a man more likely to accept this kind of violence.

"Who Would Believe Me, Anyway?": Why You Can't Pass Off His Excuses or Take the Blame for Rape

One of the worst aspects of experiencing rape is that the victimization doesn't end with the physical act. Sometimes other people will try to convince you that nothing really happened, that you won't be taken seriously, or that you should take the blame because you let things go too far. Below are some reasons that the responsibility for rape is often pushed onto the victim. None of these, however, is an excuse for predatory or violent behavior.

Being friendly. Act too cold to a guy, and you're a "bitch." Seem too nice, and you're accused of "wanting" it. If you have ever thought that you just can't get a break around guys, you're not crazy. Studies have shown that guys tend to interpret even nonverbal cues of friendliness, such as smiling, as signs that a woman wants to have sex. Just complimenting a guy can be taken as a signal that it's "okay, go" time. You don't need to become an instant ice queen in the presence of a dude. You just need to be aware that a guy may think that you have an ulterior motive in being polite when he's being pushy.

Letting a guy walk you home. It doesn't matter if he gets you all the way to the door and you make out as though your life depends on it. It's not cause for him to invite himself in. If he doesn't live there, he doesn't belong there.

Going out on a date with a guy. You agreed to dinner, not to sign away your body to him. Most people understand that a date is a social contract with no guarantees. Being the one who pays the bill doesn't give a person the right to force sex.

Staying out late. Whether it's a party, a job, or a team project at the library, being out "after hours" is often a necessity. You may have a curfew at home and under the law. This doesn't mean that after a certain hour it becomes acceptable for a guy to expect sex.

Getting high or drunk. Many date rapists will try to twist the scenario around in your mind if one of you was imbibing: "Of course you wanted it. You wouldn't have had so much to drink if you didn't want to loosen up." Or "Hey, you made the first move on me. Don't you remember?" Or "I didn't know you were passed out—I thought you were just lying there." Don't let this happen.

You could even be the one who bought him a drink or bought him shots and challenged him to a drink-off. Legally, it's up to the guy to recognize that you were beyond consent.

Dressing in a certain way. It's an unfair but common thought: "If women didn't wear short skirts and high heels, they wouldn't get raped." Don't you believe it: you can express yourself any way you want, and that includes wearing revealing clothing. Putting on a miniskirt is not an invitation for a guy to touch you or rape you. You should be aware that some guys will assume things about your sexual history based on what you wear. But it has nothing to do with what is acceptable behavior on their part.

Having a "reputation" or many past sexual partners. Unfortunately, a girl's sexual history can be used against her. Studies show that women who have more consensual sexual partners are more likely to experience sexual victimization. This doesn't mean that you're "asking for it"; it just means that you're more likely to come across a sexually aggressive guy and be in a situation where he takes things too far.

Living Through This:
Coping with a Sexual Assault

Survivors of sexual abuse can go on to lead amazing lives—Oprah Winfrey and Queen Latifah are just two examples of this. To be sure, it takes a lot of healing and hard work to get there.

The repercussions of rape aren't always clear immediately after the act. The victim will deal with a range of emotions, and won't always get a fair warning when they're about to crop up. The aftereffects one might experience include the following:

- Feeling guilty for "letting it happen"
- Being angry with yourself or the assailant
- Experiencing anxiety in one-to-one or group situations
- Having nightmares or flashbacks
- Living in fear of it happening again or of retaliation
- Feeling ashamed or humiliated that someone violated your body
- Having trouble sleeping or eating
- Experiencing severe mood swings
- Using drugs or alcohol to feel calm or numb
- Feeling insecure at formerly safe spaces, like home or school
- Wanting to harm yourself physically to relieve emotional pain
- Having trouble setting sexual boundaries or thinking that you're good for nothing but sex
- Feeling depressed or thinking that life is no longer worth living

All of these can be expected, and they can be triggered by something as simple as a guy flirting with you or a stranger brushing up against your back. If you find yourself in this situation and your feelings seem too heavy to handle alone, you need to get help from a counselor, or if you can't, at least talk to a friend. You may not want to tell your parents what happened. Sometimes a survivor feels angry because she thinks that her family should have protected her from the attack, even when that wasn't possible or her parents didn't know the guy. This is totally understandable. Dealing with these negative emotions can be difficult, but with the help of a therapist, someone at a sexual assault hotline, or a survivors' support group, a woman can move forward.

Experiencing Sexual Assault:
What to Do

Whether you're a guy's girlfriend, classmate, coworker, buddy, or acquaintance, you have a right to be respected. You can even be sexy around him yet not have your body up for grabs at all times. You are not responsible for making a guy control himself or feel sexually satisfied. This means that you never have to consent to anything that doesn't feel right, even if you're in a relationship with a guy now or used to be.

Sexual activity should never involve pushes, threats, or coercion. *Always* speak up if a guy does any of these. In most states, the law requires that there be verbal consent, which means that one person asks the other one if it's okay, and the other person responds with a clear *yes*. The word *no* is enough. You may be tempted to joke about it ("Put that mess away!") or be polite. Don't. He needs to know how serious you are.

Women shouldn't have to take responsibility for not getting assaulted; nevertheless, there are some things you can do to lower the odds of it happening to you. First, it's important to walk with confidence, whether you're on the street or in the school hallway. Take your iPod off and be aware of your surroundings! Listen to your feelings of unease or fear; they mean you are picking up on cues in the environment. Rapists report that the most common tactics they use on a victim are trying to isolate a girl physically, building her up with flattery if they think she has low self-esteem, catching her off guard, and violating her personal space with accidental touches or stares. These things are intended to make you think that he's less threatening than he really is, so always be aware of a guy who is trying to take advantage of your trust in him to get you in a situation in which you'll be unable to get help or defend yourself.

On a smaller scale, be sure to point out to your guy friends that sexual violence is not a punch line or a metaphor. A guy who says, "Dude, I just got raped in that geology exam!" might not understand how insensitive this statement is. However, ignorance is not an excuse. Tell him "How do you think that would make someone who has actually been sexually assaulted feel to hear that? There's a good chance that you're within earshot of a girl who has experienced it firsthand but is too afraid or ashamed to talk about it."

👍 What to **SAY** to His **LIES**:

✓ "Stop."

✓ "No."

✓ "I don't want to do this."

✓ "You need to leave."

✓ "Get off me."

✓ "Get away from me."

✓ "This is hurting me."

✓ "I don't like this."

✓ "I've changed my mind. This has to stop."

✓ "You don't have the right to do this to me."

✓ "I said **no**, so you have to stop."

✓ "This is rape."

☞ What to **DO** if You Already Bought the **LIE:**

If you are a victim of sexual violence, the first thing you need
to do is acknowledge that it happened. The second is to make
sure that you do not blame yourself for it. This is so importance
that we'll say it twice: **Never blame yourself**. And don't let yourself believe any of his excuses for victimizing you, like "I wasn't
going to do anything, but then you go and wear that top."

Even if you didn't explicitly say **no** or tell him to stop, it can
still be rape. Sometimes you cannot resist physically or say
something because it's not safe. (For instance, he threatened
your life or someone else's, or he used a weapon.) Consensual
sex that turned violent or made you unable to resist counts,
too, and it doesn't matter whether you hooked up with him
first. You also are not able to consent legally if you're a
certain age or were intoxicated or using drugs.

The next step is to get to a safe place, away from the
attacker. Never EVER let the attacker take you to a second
location. The chances of you being seriously hurt or killed
skyrocket once he moves you from one place to another.

After a sexual assault, you will probably feel physically
and mentally exhausted. Your first instinct will probably
be to clean yourself. That's perfectly normal, but it's
absolutely vital that you don't. There is only one
opportunity to collect evidence of the attack that can
be used against your assailant later on. If you wash it away,
that opportunity is lost. You should be examined by a doctor
ASAP. This is also to make sure that you weren't injured in
any way that isn't immediately obvious and to get treatment
to prevent a possible STI. Getting a medical exam after a rape,

or a rape kit, does not mean that you don't have to report the crime to the police. It's impossible to tell how you'll feel one minute, hour, day, or year after your assault. Having a full report of what happened, along with physical proof, is good insurance for a strong case should it be necessary. Immediately after the attack, go to the emergency room. Regardless of how you feel, **do not** do any of the following:

- Shower or bathe
- Change your clothes
- Brush your teeth
- Douche
- Use hand sanitizer
- Scrub or clip your nails

If you're under 18, you're allowed to get help from the police or a healthcare provider without parental consent, but it's best to seek assistance accompanied by a friend, a family member, or some other adult in whom you trust. You can also request a victim advocate who will speak on your behalf. You'll need to tell the doctor about everything you've ingested recently—even if it's illegal—and who gave it to you.

If the sex was unprotected, you should be tested for STIs and get access to emergency contraception. If force was used, ask about when to follow up with a gynecologist to make sure that no damage was done internally.

Your recovery process might include pursuing justice against your assailant. It might take some time for you to figure out what you want to do, but you need to know that you have rights. There are local rape crisis centers in nearly every community—call the National Sexual Assault Hotline at 1-800-656-HOPE to find one near you.

Q&A

Q: If I am sexually assaulted, do I really have to report it?

A: No, by law you don't have to report it. However, you should know that by reporting it, you will be helping other girls to avoid your experience in the future. Rapists rarely rape just once. Although it's not your responsibility to stop this guy from raping or sexually assaulting another girl, it can be healing for you to know that you've helped to get this guy off the street.

Q: I know a guy who was falsely accused of rape, and it totally ruined his life. Don't a lot of girls cry wolf?

A: It happens, but it's far outweighed by the number of rapists who are unprosecuted. Because men tend to have physical power over women, it's important that a guy gets a girl's explicit consent every time he has any physical contact, even if it means making things a little awkward for a minute.

Q: Can a guy be raped?

A: Yes. Although men are typically the aggressors in sexual assaults, they can be victims, too, regardless of their sexual orientation. Sexual assault is not about desire, it's about violence, power, control, and humiliation. Every person has the right to say *no* to any kind of sexual contact, even if he or she first consented but then had a change of mind.

Q: I was sexually abused when I was younger. Does this mean that I'm not pure or that I'll be more likely to be assaulted again?

A: Purity has nothing to do with it. Don't ever let anyone tell you that you're damaged or not whole because of what happened to you. The person who did this took a lot from you, but what you still have—in addition to your strength and your spirit—is the right to define your sex life any way you want. You may choose not to have sex for a long time. When you do, you deserve for it to be consensual and with partners who love and respect you.

LIE #16

"You need someone to keep you in line."

DATING VIOLENCE AND THE SURPRISING FORMS OF "LOVE" THAT ARE REALLY ABUSE

🐾 Other Ways He **MIGHT** Say It

- ✗ "You deserved it."
- ✗ "You pushed me to get that angry at you."
- ✗ "You need to be taught a lesson."
- ✗ "If you leave, I'll kill myself."
- ✗ "Love should be intense, so it's normal for things to get physical."
- ✗ "You're stupid. You're crazy."
- ✗ "No one in your family loves you like I do."
- ✗ "It's either me or your friends and your family."

☞ The **TRUTH**:

Like the last chapter, this is one that we really wish we
didn't have to write. But more girls hear these abusive lies
than you'd expect. Almost one-third of teens report being
victims of emotional and physical abuse by romantic
partners. And one in five girls has been in a violent relationship or has been threatened with violence by a partner.

In a normal loving relationship, a guy will make you feel
great about yourself, even on days when you're at your worst.
Sometimes even guys who are abusers can make you feel this
way at the start. A boy might begin by showing you more
attention than any guy ever has. You might not even be sure
that you're into him. But he's persistent, always hanging
around. The fact that he won't take no for answer might
be flattering, a sign that he really is so into you.

Soon, though, his possessiveness turns to jealousy. He
treats you like a possession, trying to get control over what
you do or who you hang out with. Or he's unpredictable:
adorable one moment, then raging at you the next and telling
you it's your fault that he can't get a handle on his temper.

Some people think that if you aren't married or dependent
on a guy for money or to raise kids, you can't be a victim of
partner violence. The stereotypical idea of an abused woman
seems so far from who you are: a strong, smart girl. You just
have silly spats with your guy—yeah, they get heated, but
eventually they blow over if you just don't do something stupid
to set him off, right? Wrong. It's every bit as serious as adult
abuse. And it may be even more destructive to you, because

you are new to relationships and are learning to distinguish the boundaries between a healthy relationship and an abusive one. A lot of what you're going through now as a teen can make it hard for you to recognize or leave a destructive relationship.

What Counts as Abuse and Who Goes Through It

The first thing you should know is that no one is immune. Nearly one in three women has suffered from intimate partner abuse. It's not just the "weak" girls, the "dumb" ones, the ones who "deserve" it, or any other stereotype. Violence against women affects all ethnicities, economic levels, religions, and sexual orientations. And it's affecting girls at younger ages all the time.

Although abuse is a common reality, talking about it isn't. Less than 25 percent of teens say they've spoken to their parents about dating violence. That creates a lot of misunderstanding about what qualifies as a harmful relationship. When you're new to dating in general, you might not know where the line is between a comfortable, supportive partnership and one that veers into abuse. A guy may pass off bad behavior as "what everyone goes through." If your parents haven't told you or shown you what's really healthy, you could assume that it's what happens in all relationships.

At the same time, guys are getting negative messages about how to treat women. When they see celebrities, sports icons, and politicians who treat women badly still enjoy hero status, a lot of them might think that it's actually good to abuse or control women. Much of the entertainment in our culture is based on violence—and specifically violence against women—in video games, music lyrics, and movies. One recent study showed that the incidence of violence against teen girls on TV has increased by 400 percent in the past five years. When all we see are examples of women as victims, it can lead boys to think that this is our only role.

If a guy believes this, he's less likely to get into a relationship in which he loves and respects a girl. Instead, it's all about power and control. Abusers may say they love or care about their partners, but the real goal is to dominate, humiliate, and isolate their girlfriends and wives.

Physical Abuse

Physical abuse is the form that you're probably most familiar with. It refers to any incident in which someone uses his body to hurt yours—for instance, by hitting, slapping, pushing, kicking, choking, biting, grabbing, or slamming you against a wall. Even a light touch can result in serious harm: a light push is a big deal if you fall down the stairs.

Mental and Emotional Abuse

Emotional abuse is the category of abuse that most girls tend to brush off as no big deal, but it can be just as dangerous and hurtful as any physical act. It occurs when a guy tries to get control over your thoughts and your actions by demeaning you—and it's no exaggeration to call it brainwashing.

He might tell you not to think about anyone other than him, that you're worthless or going nowhere without him, or that you don't even exist as a person outside the relationship. He might also say that your family doesn't really love you and that he's the only one in your life who does. He can take it further by isolating you from your friends, acting possessive or jealous of them, and trying to control where you go and what you do. Accusing you of ulterior motives when you hang out with male friends ("You can't be friends with a guy. They all just want to hook up with you— you must want it, too, if you're still buddies.") and telling you what to wear around other people (so that you won't "turn them on") are abusive behaviors.

An abuser might also blame you for the mistakes he makes, such as cheating, or for getting angry in general. He could threaten to hurt you, himself, or someone else physically if you don't do what he says. Simply looking at you in ways that scare you counts as intimidation.

Verbal Abuse

Verbal abuse occurs when a guy says things to put you down or criticize you. A quarter of teenage girls in relationships have reported being verbally abused by their boyfriends. Many of the lies we've outlined so far in the book qualify, such as name-calling (e.g., ugly, slut, whore, worthless, stupid). The tone he uses also matters: he can yell in a way that scares or humiliates you even when the content of what he's saying isn't hurtful.

Sexual Abuse

Sexual abuse occurs when a guy, whether it's your committed boyfriend or just a onetime hookup, coerces you into any kind of sexual contact or forces it on you violently. Many guys do this along with emotional abuse. They may guilt-trip you, telling you that if you loved them, you'd do it for them, or that they'll leave if you won't do a certain thing. One in three girls report being sexually abused by a boyfriend.

Forcing you to have unprotected sex or not use birth control is abusive, too. A guy may even try to get you pregnant on purpose or against your will. It's called pregnancy coercion, and one study found that one in five young women has experienced it, and that your chances of getting pregnant are doubled if you experience sexual or physical abuse on top of coercion.

Digital Abuse

You might associate cyber harassment with "mean girls" and bullies, but your partner can do it, too. Name-calling, ridiculing, forcing you to give up passwords, pressuring you to send naked photos and videos or have digital sex, trying to monitor and control you—all of these activities are forms of abuse, whether it's online or by cell phone.

One of the most common but unrecognized forms of digital abuse is excessive texting and calling. Almost a quarter of teens in relationships say that they have communicated with their partners by cell phone or computer hourly between midnight and 5:00 AM. Because we're all so wired to our gadgets, you might not realize that you're being smothered by obsessive contact. So if he's checking in on you every ten minutes, pressuring you to report your location every hour or demanding that you always be available on IM, it's not proof of a good connection. It's a sign of abuse.

Economic Abuse

Economic abuse is less of a factor for young women who are still dependent on their parents for money. Still, it's a serious issue. For partners who live together, it involves one person tightly restricting the other person's access to joint finances or making him or her account for every penny spent—even when it's the latter's money. Forcing you to miss your after-school job to be with him or sabotaging your job by showing up unannounced is also a form of economic abuse. Stealing money, especially to fund a drug and alcohol habit, obviously counts as well.

Understanding the Abuse Cycle

You don't have to experience all of these forms at once or for a long period of time for any one of them to qualify as abuse. Often, a guy's cruelty is not constant, but rather intermittent, with episodes that can be as short as seconds or as lengthy as years.

Abuse starts with tension building, a stage in which the guy picks fights for no reason and tries to make you believe that you can't do anything right. You're not sure what you did to deserve this hostility, but you do whatever you can to please him. Otherwise, the situation could get out of hand at any moment, it seems. Eventually you will be blamed for "slipping up." Maybe you answer dozens of check-in calls a day, but the one time you don't, he tracks you down at home or at sports practice.

That's when there is an explosion of violence. Yelling and screaming is a common way in which a guy might lose his temper. There may be hitting, punching, slapping, kicking, or forcing sex, but the situation doesn't have to get that heated or even physical to be abusive and manipulative. Simply calling you a slut and accusing you of cheating, with no proof, or threatening to hurt you counts as abuse. Typically, he'll pick a time that he knows the two of you will be alone together to do this. Abusers save the worst of themselves for their partners; they choose a time that is convenient for them to take out their anger on their target when they can't be called on it by a third party.

After he acts out, the abuser may feel guilty. This is not because he feels bad for hurting you. He's realizing that what he did was wrong and that he could have been caught doing it. He might apologize or try to make it up to you somehow, triggering what's known as a "honeymoon period." An apology may come in words or through flowers, gifts, or physical affection. He may also try to shift the blame for his outburst onto something like stress or the influence of drugs and alcohol.

This is one of the most critical stages, because it impacts whether you'll stay with him in the future. You might feel a lot of pressure to work things out, especially if he promises never to do it again. He could say that he'll show you he's changing and wants to prove it to you. Often, however, abusers couch their "sorry" with a warning of future action, like "I wouldn't have to do this if you weren't so [fill in the blank]," which subtly tells you that it will happen again if you don't do what he says. The honeymoon period can last for a while, but eventually he'll find an excuse to get annoyed or angry with you again. This ratchets up the tension and puts you back where you started, waiting for the other shoe to drop.

Why It's So Hard to Leave an Abuser—and Why You Absolutely Have to Do It

Wonder just how damaging and powerful abuse can be? It can make a bright, confident girl say things she'd never expect, like these statements:

"He promised it will never happen again, and I have faith in him."

"He didn't mean it; he just snapped."

"He made one mistake—how could I just dump him?"

"I'm the strong one, and I have an obligation to help him."

"Other girls get treated a lot worse than this."

"He was so sad and really meant it when he apologized. He just loves me too much."

"He got me a gift to make up for it, which was so sweet."

"He wouldn't have to do it if I didn't make him feel so bad, so I'm to blame as well."

All of these statements are things that victims of abuse commonly tell themselves or other people to rationalize a partner's bad behavior. A lot of people don't understand why a girl would put up with this, since every second she stays with him she's at risk of serious harm, even death. It's important to understand how warped your mind can get when you feel isolated and hurt by the person you love but are so willing to believe his excuses or that he'll change. That's why nearly 80 percent of girls who have been victims of physical abuse in their dating relationships continue to date their abuser.

You'd think that being married to an abuser would make you more tied to him than just dating him. But getting out of a relationship can be very difficult for teen girls because they could have a lot to lose socially if they don't have a boyfriend at school. Sometimes having a boyfriend, even a mean one, feels better than having none at all. If your guy is popular or well liked by your family, he could use his charm against you. Some abusers will say that you need this relationship to fit in or be accepted—without him, other people will hate you, or he'll see to it that they do. You might worry about what will happen if your friends are forced to choose sides should you break up. If you've been intimate, you might fear that he'll spread rumors about you.

You may believe that you're the abuser's only hope and that love can transform him. You don't want to give up on him, you just want the violence to stop, so you think, "If I can just stick with him and get through this, he'll change." Abusers are often really skilled at making you think that you're responsible for their mental and physical states. This kind of guy will even tell you that if you leave, he'll fall apart or kill himself. Then you'd be responsible for abandoning and destroying him.

None of this makes the violence right or excusable. All of it is a sign that things will get worse if you don't end the relationship immediately.

Beyond Bruises:
What Can Happen to You If You Stay

About 70 percent of girls in abusive relationships experience physical injuries, and 9 percent of them have been to the emergency room because of abuse at the hands of a dating partner. Studies show that if you're in a physically abusive relationship, you're at a greater risk of contracting HIV or STIs in general, and of becoming pregnant without planning it because sex is forced on you. Men are much more likely than women to kill or injure their partners over jealousy.

Aside from the physical injuries, the mental and emotional effects can be just as devastating. Experts think that your brain actually changes in response to this toxic treatment. Because you're always on high alert, you could be prone to emotional disorders, easily startled, hypervigilant, and anxious. You're also at increased risk of developing a substance abuse problem in order to cope, and you're more likely to attempt suicide than girls who are not abused.

Getting out ASAP is critical if you want to be in a healthy relationship in the future. You need time to rebuild your self-esteem, otherwise you risk seeking out abusers in the future and experiencing patterns of abuse and negative relationships for life.

The Ex Factor: The Fatal Flaw in Seeing Your Guy "One Last Time"

YOU MAY WANT TO GIVE YOUR GUY one more chance to prove himself or make up after a brief breakup. Don't. It could cost your life. One in five teenage girls who have been in an abusive relationship has been threatened with violence if she breaks things off, and dozens of guys each year make good on this promise.

It happened to Arizona high-schooler Kaity Sudberry at age 17. She was murdered by her ex-boyfriend only one week after her parents tried to get protection from the authorities from his harassing and abusive behavior after their breakup. Unfortunately, he was able to track her down, because Arizona didn't grant people who are or were only dating each other the same protection under law as those who live with, are married to, are blood related to, or are pregnant by an abusive partner. As a result of her death, legislators created Kaity's Law, which aims to protect young single girls from the same tragic fate as its namesake.

Abuse in the Spotlight

IN 2008, PHOTOS WERE RELEASED TO THE PUBLIC that showed music superstar Rihanna with bruises, allegedly the result of physical abuse by her equally famous boyfriend, Chris Brown. Just seeing her split lip and her gorgeous face speckled with black-and-blue marks was enough to make your skin crawl, right? Even more shocking, though, was how many young girls weren't on the victim's side. Many of her biggest fans believed that Rihanna "was asking for it."

It took Rihanna courageously setting the record straight months after the fact to finally change minds. "This happened to me," she said in her first interview after the incident. "It can happen to anyone. He was definitely my first big love." In the days after her public statement, calls to domestic violence centers went up 59 percent, with a 72 percent increase among teens, which suggested that her openness led to more girls feeling comfortable seeking help and realizing that they no longer had to suffer in silence.

"Domestic violence is a big secret," Rihanna said. "No kid goes around and lets people know their parents fight. Teen-age girls can't tell their parents that their boyfriend beat them up. You don't dare let your neighbor know that you fight. It's one of the things we [women] will hide, because it's embarrassing. My story was broadcast all over the world for people to see, and they have followed every step of my recovery."

Dating Violence: What to Do

Understand that you deserve respect, caring, and love from a guy. Bruises, insults, and harassment are never proof of this. No guy is allowed to control or manipulate you physically, mentally, or emotionally just because he is your boyfriend. And you never have to consent to sexual activity just because everyone else thinks a guy is a "good kid" or because you've been together forever.

You might need to proceed more slowly than you think in a relationship in order to figure out whether it's healthy and right for you. This means having plenty of space from a guy as you're getting to know each other so that you have the ability to tune in to what doesn't feel right. This will help you to develop an instinct for what is healthy and balanced. Don't be afraid to set boundaries that other girls won't. Sharing secrets and doing anything with your body that you don't feel ready for is never a good idea, no matter how many of your friends do it.

Think twice about anyone who wants to keep you from your support system—your family and friends. It is completely okay—actually, vital—to want time to yourself and to talk with other people about your relationship. You need outsiders to act as a mirror and a compass, orienting you when you're going in the wrong direction. If your friends and your family are telling you that they don't like this guy or that he's bringing out the worst in you, listen to them.

If anything frightens you, write it down or tell someone, and save all messages or posts from a guy who seems even vaguely wrong or threatening. If his behavior scares you, you always have the right to end a relationship no matter how "silly" the reason seems to him or anyone else. Regardless of how calm a guy seems in public and how kind he was when making amends, he can still be violent and abusive in private without anyone else knowing.

What to **SAY** to His **LIES**:

✓ "I want respect out of a relationship. You are not giving it, so I want out."

✓ "I'm allowed to live my life without you constantly monitoring me. We are two different people, and you don't have control over me."

✓ "You do not have the right to treat me like this. It's abusive and illegal."

✓ "I love you, but I'm not going to give you my passwords. You don't need them, and I don't need yours."

✓ "I don't care if you say it will never happen again. That is a chance I cannot take."

✓ "What you're doing is abusive. It has to stop now."

✓ "It doesn't matter if you're sorry or if you think it's no big deal. I don't like this, and I don't deserve to be hurt like this."

✓ "You cannot talk to me like that. Even if it's just words, it counts as abuse."

✓ "This might be your idea of love, but it's not mine."

✓ "I don't care if you were drunk or stressed out. What you did was wrong."

☞ What to **DO** if You Already Bought the **LIE:**

Experiencing abuse can be shocking the first time it happens, especially if you think of yourself as a strong girl. No matter how it occurs, you need to know that it's not deserved, it's never your fault, and a better life awaits you away from him.

Abuse almost never happens just once; few guys who are aggressive ever stop when they say they will. You must not believe that he simply can't control his temper. If this were true, he would lash out at everyone he comes in contact with. He doesn't—he is choosing you. (Also, if he couldn't control his temper, he'd lash out at you in public instead of waiting till he gets you alone.) This is proof that he is not a loving person. You have to leave him before you get hurt anymore. If you are scared to end a relationship, that in itself is a sign that it must end.

The abuse may get worse when you try to break off the relationship, but there are things you can do to protect yourself. First, don't break up in person—you need physical distance to be safe. Tell your friends and your family that you are going to do it, and make sure they check up on you or are nearby afterward. Don't explain to him more than once your intent or your reasons for ending the relationship. Just say that it's over and that he is never allowed to contact you again. If you fear he'll come after you, make sure you are protected and always with another person in a public space. Also, have a cell phone ready to call for help. If you ever feel you're in immediate danger, call 911 or the National Teen Dating Abuse Helpline at 866-331-9474.

You may continue to care about a guy you dated who was abusive, even many years after you split up. But it's better for you to keep your distance. Cutting him out of your life completely is not bitchy. It's self-preservation. If you have any reason to think he could get violent, you must avoid all contact with him. You shouldn't even go to the door if he comes to your house. You might need to look into getting a restraining order against him if he continues to contact you. If you're under 18, you may need the help of an adult to get one. This can be a friend or a relative, who is sometimes referred to as a guardian ad litem. Another option is a protective order, in which the court says it's illegal for the abuser to harm you, come near you, or contact you.

You also have options at school. Make sure that if you attend the same one, you will be protected by the staff and the teachers—it's your right under the law. You can also insist on having a friend or a school staff member walk with you between classes and give you a ride home so he's not able to corner you while you wait somewhere alone.

After a breakup, it's normal to feel drained. You could think you've lost part of yourself, that you're alone, and that no one can understand what you're going through. Feeling lost without him is particularly common if he used to make decisions for you, even if you knew they were wrong. You may need to seek counseling to deal with these emotions, or it might help to write down why you needed to end the relationship, in order to convince yourself that it was the right decision. Above all, give yourself time to make peace with what happened.

Q&A

Q: Can a guy be abused?

A: Absolutely, though it's less common. Guys can be just as traumatized by violence, even name-calling, as girls. All abuse should be taken seriously, regardless of the victim's gender.

Q: My best friend is in a relationship with a guy who hurts her. I've told her over and over that she has to leave him, but she refuses. I don't know what to do. How can I get her out of this?

A: It's great that you're such a proactive friend. Your role is to make sure she knows that you're always there for her whenever she wants to talk and that you're worried about her self esteem or that she may get hurt. Be as specific as you can about what changes you've seen in her from the abuse. If your friend is in danger, you need to tell an adult, such as a coach, a teacher, a counselor, or a parent, who can get her help. You also need to give her a heads-up that you're doing this so she's aware it's coming and has the opportunity to do it herself first.

Finally, don't place conditions on your friendship and support. It may take several tries for her to leave, and your being around to listen and help is terrifically important.

Q: My boyfriend told me that his dad frequently hit his mom when he was growing up. Now I'm worried that he could be violent with me one day. How likely is it that this could happen?

A: Even though it wouldn't be fair to judge him by his family's abuse, you should know that teens who witness family violence are more prone to violence themselves. They may commit partner abuse, be abused, suffer from depression or anxiety, and have substance abuse problems. This doesn't mean that it will happen to him, but you need to be aware of the possibility and help him to seek support from a counselor. Your love and support can be a big help for him, but it's always your responsibility to look out for yourself first. If he ever shows signs of abusive behavior toward you, you need to leave him and seek help on your own.

LIE #17

"I'll love you forever."

AND OTHER PROMISES HE JUST CAN'T KEEP

🐎 Other Ways He **MIGHT** Say It

✗ "Love conquers all."

✗ "I love you more than anyone else ever will."

✗ "We were meant to be together."

✗ "I'll never leave you."

👉 The **TRUTH**:

You're probably wondering why we put this lie at the end. We saved the best for last, of course. And we do mean the best.

Someday a guy will try to express to you how fabulous and incandescent he thinks you are by whispering the three most powerful words known to humanity: "I love you." He'll really mean it, too.

It's just that today probably isn't that day. Let us explain.

Guys will use and abuse the L-word to get what they want. Take them at their L-word and you might make compromises and decisions that aren't good for you: staying in your hometown instead of moving to the city you've always dreamed of living in, getting married before you're allowed to do things like vote or drink, or not using a condom.

We aren't saying that there won't be guys who say it and mean it, and that you can be really, really young and be in love, but we are telling you to look carefully at **who** says it and **when**. Is it at a moment when he wants something from you?

Fact is, he might even be confused about what love is, so now you are left to figure out your feelings **and** his! Below are a few things that he might really be thinking of when he claims it's all about **amour**.

Lust Lie #1: "I Love Your Body"

The L-word bomb has been dropped at many an inappropriate time by guys throughout history. (For example, when a guy hears "I got my STI test results: Negative," next comes "Ah, I *love* you, baby! Now let me show it with my penis.") But nowhere is it more common than in the 0.4 seconds before a guy has an orgasm. Some of this can be chalked up to a case of mistaken identity—a boy who's new to dating and mating could innocently confuse lust with love. But most guys know that girls tend to prefer to have sex when they're in love with a guy and want to feel loved back. All they have to do to get action from some women is to say the L-word, or even "I think I'm falling in love with you," and they're golden. Others take it to a whole new level of jerkitude and deliberately pretend to care about you until they get bored with the booty and disappear.

Believe it or not, you could feel the same if your hookups are molten-lava hot. But this isn't love. It might just be great sex. That's why there's a danger in assuming that amazing sex is a sign of great relationship potential. Every time that it is actually good with a guy, you'll have even higher expectations for the emotional part because you connect so well physically. The moment the chemistry or his penis go south—and at least one will, at some point—your idea of über-passionate love comes crashing down around you.

Lust Lie #2: "I Love Being in Love"

If we could create an online dating ad for the type of guy who typically says this, it would read: "Incurable romantic desperately searching for a cure." Whereas other players pretend to be mortal enemies of romance, this dude is so into the idea of love he's like a Nicholas Sparks novel come to life. Everything is dramatic and idealized, played really large on a screen. And it's all fiction, of course.

Yes, even guys' brains can get polluted by fairy tales. Most boys who suffer from this do so because they lack the knowledge about how relationships really work. For example, there is the guy who does great the first two or three weeks of a relationship, then it goes downhill because from that point on *you* have to do some work or make some accommodations.

He'd rather just stare at your eyes all day, even if he doesn't really remember what color they are at the end of it. After all, the object of his affection isn't you and all your quirks; it's love. And love is perfect. You're not (and that's a good thing), but that could be why he eventually freaks and leaves: he realized that you're a human being who occasionally snorts when you laugh. Love would never do that!

Lust Lie #3
"I Love the Idea of You"

This dude knows that you're a great catch on paper—maybe you both come from good families or hang out with the same people. He thinks you're cute. He says you're hilarious. Many girls are guilty of this, too, when they get to know a guy who *seems* like he should be right up their alley. Sometimes, if you can't think of a good enough reason *not* to go for someone, you think that's a reason to say, "Okey-dokey, I'm up for it!" Then you're forced to cling to superficial stuff, like having one big hobby or quirk in common. You can tell yourself, "But we love the same ba-a-a-and. And we both crack up over Demetri Martin albums!" That doesn't mean that you love each other. You love him only as a reflection of yourself.

This is a problem when you don't let your real self show in these cool-in-theory relationships. You might fudge an interest you don't really feel so as not to rock the boat with a guy. This fake love happens a lot when you're young because you're trying on lots of different personalities to figure out which one is right for you. So whoever you go for now might not be compatible with the person you will be in six months. And that's how a guy can make the mistake of falling for you, because you're both environmental activists today, but no one can predict if either one of you will still be green crusaders in the next nine months, let alone nine days.

Lust Lie #4: "I'll Love You Until It's No Longer Convenient to Do It"

Your introductory experience with love can be the most intense of your life. It can feel raw, potent, or electric. So of course the first guy whose name you draw hearts and stars around when you're supposed to be paying attention in class is going to have a special role in your life. It is hard to believe that there will be other loves after him. It is hard to believe that he may not be "the one." But really, what are the odds that our soul mate is the person who is sitting one row over in homeroom?

You'll probably have more than one career in your lifetime, and you'll be friends with hundreds of people on social networking sites, some of whom you'll never meet. Why wouldn't you also have a few other love affairs before you find the person you'll want to be with at age 80?

Lust Lie #5: "I Love You Because I Hate Myself"

Nothing turns a "good-enough-for-now" guy into someone long-term more than discovering he's got potential. Convincing yourself that you need to stick around to change someone leads us to one of the biggest love lies we tell ourselves: "I love the person you could be with my help."

Let's back up the crazy train here, girls. Boys are not your personal remodeling projects. If you become fixated on guys you want to makeover emotionally, the only person you need to fix is yourself, starting with your Florence Nightingale fetish. No matter how hard you try to nurse a guy back to health or out of mediocrity, you're going to have to keep putting up with increasingly crappy behavior that you'll never be able to control—like the smashed guy who shows up at your door at 5:00 AM, stinking of Everclear and weepy with apologies and promises that he's really, really gonna cut back tomorrow; the cheater who says you're the only woman he could see himself with long-term—he just needs to get his three girls on the side out of his system first; or the boy who is stuck on you and also in a deep depression but refuses to talk to a counselor about it.

Each one may give you his everything. But that doesn't mean it's enough for you. It's only living proof that love doesn't conquer all— not even the pure, patient version of love that you have to offer.

Is It for Real?

So when *can* you believe the word "love" when you hear it?

Many young people expect to achieve relationship utopia quickly and without working at it, but it takes effort to keep even the best bonds strong. First of all, you have to find someone who thinks that you're great as you are and that you're great for him. That requires a mix of things you have in common, like values (how you think about spirituality, politics, family, money, and so on), and at least a couple of things you enjoy doing together, beyond knocking boots. It also takes a certain kind of emotional connection that you can't put on paper.

Research shows that there's a difference between someone who would be a good guy for you to date now versus one to be with for the long haul. For example, he's the cheerleader who says, "Go Team You!" when you announce you want to join the Peace Corps and work in Papua New Guinea, even if it means time apart from each other. Or maybe he helps you to live up to the responsibilities and follow through on promises you've made, holding your hand at the hospital while you're waiting for your mom to get out of surgery, or going to yet another friend's party with you, even if it's the seventeenth of the summer.

However you decide on what kind of love you are looking for, and however you learn about the different *kinds* of love you can experience, what we can tell you is that you will get better at really knowing when the person saying he loves you means it wholeheartedly.

True Love: What to Do

Take your time defining what love really looks and feels like for you, what kind you want to give and to receive. If you're one of those girls who can't envision getting a tattoo because you change your mind on the design every week, it's safe to say that you shouldn't commit to loving one person forever and ever at this moment. That's cool, though. You have years to sort this stuff out!

As you start to figure out what your heart truly desires, you might find that your vocabulary changes a little as you articulate what you want. You should know that changing your mind is not a bad thing; in fact, you may discover that taking time to spell out

Words to Love By
"Men always want to be a woman's first love. Women like to be a man's last romance."
—Oscar Wilde

what you *don't* want can help you refine your definition, even if it's not that much fun.

In the meantime, it's up to you to be a little skeptical of guys who profess their love to you now. You might have to sniff out a guy's camouflaged lust and put the brakes on things sexually before you get hurt. You also have to question whether guys can really follow through on everything they promise. Just because they truly want to be there forever doesn't mean that they can or will. And you shouldn't put off doing cool stuff with your life in the interim. On the flip side, don't let fear of ending up alone tie you to a lackluster guy just because you've been together since you were kids or he was your first love. Always ask yourself if you really want him to be your boyfriend, or if you just want to be able to tell people, "I have a boyfriend!" There *is* a difference.

👍 What to **SAY** to His **LIES**:

✓ "Don't you mean you love my body?"

✓ "Forever? I'm not sure I can count that high."

✓ "Let's just focus on what we really feel in the here and now."

👉 What to **DO** if You Already Bought the **LIE**:

You thought you found a guy who was good for you because he said the word **love**, but it turns out he's an emotional infant. It hurts like hell to realize that he didn't want you for your personality, and that sometimes people aren't who you thought they were.

On the other hand, maybe you've paid too much attention to friends telling you, "Stop being so picky—he loves you!" and as a result you've talked yourself into a relationship you think you **should** want. So what you should do is stop letting people tell you what you can or can't have, what you should or shouldn't do. If you get the funny feeling that you're settling for less (while at the same time you're dying to explore the bigger picture), you have to give yourself a shot to find what else is out there. This means freeing your guy to do the same. True, there's the possibility that he might not be waiting if and when you come back, but it's better than staying together for the wrong reasons.

Regardless, now you're left with a big case of the blues. Know this, though: your temporary situation—being single and miserable about it or dating crap guys as though it's your destiny—is definitely not permanent. Studies show that people recover more easily and quickly from breakups than they predict they will. You're a resilient creature. You **will** bounce back. And when you turn 18 or 28, we swear you'll be able to say, "I can't believe I ever thought I could be in love with someone like that!"

In any case, you'll find that sometimes a little solitude is a great gift. It lets you figure out what you want, and realize that you can't just sit there and wait for it to come to you. You have to step up and take responsibility for your love life. Be okay with messing up and occasionally going out with a dud here or there. Every step away from what you don't want or need is a move toward what you deserve.

REFERENCES

The Alan Guttmacher Institute. *Sharing Responsibility: Women, Society and Abortion Worldwide.* New York: AGI, 1999.

Basile, K.C. et al, "Prevalence and characteristics of sexual violence victimization." *Violence and Victims* 22(4) (2007): 437–448.

Basile, K.C., "Prevalence of wife rape and other intimate partner sexual coercion in a nationally representative sample of women." *Violence and Victims* 17(5) (2002): 511–524.

Basso, Michael J. *The Underground Guide to Teenage Sexuality.* Minneapolis: Sagebrush Corporation, 2003.

Bell, Ruth. *Changing Bodies, Changing Lives: Expanded Third Edition: A Book for Teens on Sex and Relationships.* New York: Three Rivers Press, 1998.

Boston Women's Health Collective. *Our Bodies, Ourselves; Updated and Expanded for the 90s.* Gloucester, Ma: Peter Smith Publisher, 2005.

Celum, C. et al, "Effect of acyclovir on HIV-1 acquisition in herpes simplex virus type 2 seropositive women and men who have sex with men: a randomized, double blind, placebo-controlled trial." *Lancet* 371 (2008): 2109–19.

Centers for Disease Control and Prevention, "Youth Risk Behavior Surveillance—United States. 2005. Surveillance Summaries, 2006." *Morbidity and Mortality Weekly Report* 55 (2006): SS–5.

Cole, Joanna. *Asking About Sex and Growing Up: A Question-and-Answer Book for Boys and Girls.* New York: HarperCollins: 1988.

Corinna, Heather. *S.E.X.: The All-You-Need-To-Know Progressive Sexuality Guide to Get You Through High School and College.* Cambridge, MA: 2007.

Daling, J.R. et al, "Risk of Breast Cancer Among Young Women: relationship to induced abortion." *Journal of the National Cancer Institute* 86 (1994): 1584–1592.

de Vincezi, I., "A longitudinal study if human immunodeficiency virus transmission by heterosexual partners." *New England Journal of Medicine* 331 (1994): 341–46.

Dominik, R., "Male condom evaluation: statistical considerations for equivalence studies and extrapolating breakage and slippage to pregnancy rates," presented at NIH/FDA Workshop on Contraceptive Efficacy and STD Prevention: Issues in the Design of Clinical Trials. Bethesda, MD, USA, April 6–8, 1994.

Douglas, J. et al, "Screening for HSV-2 infection in STD clinics and beyond: a few answers but more questions." *Sexually Transmitted Diseases* 36 (2009): 729–31.

Elliott, D. M. et al, "Adult sexual assault: prevalence, symptomatology, and sex differences in the general population. *Journal of Traumatic Stress* 17(3) (2004): 203–211.

Fisher. B. S. et al, "The sexual victimization of college women." Washington: Department of Justice, National Institute of Justice (2000). Publication No. NCJ 182369.

Freeman, E. E. et al, "Herpes simplex virus 2 infection increases HIV acquisition in men and women: systematic review and meta-analysis of longitudinal studies." *AIDS* 20 (2006): 73–83.

Geisler, W. M. et al, "Health insurance coverage, health care-seeking behaviors, and genital chlamydia infection prevalence in sexually active young adults." *Sexually Transmitted Diseases* 33 (2006): 389–96.

Harris, Robie H. *It's Perfectly Normal: Changing Bodies, Growing Up, Sex, and Sexual Health.* Cambridge, MA: Candlewick Press, 2004.

Henshaw, S.K., "The Incidence of Abortion Worldwide," *International Family Planning Perspectives,* 25 (1999): S30–S38.

Hoover, K. et al, "Low rates of both asymptomatic chlamydia screening and diagnostic testing of young women in US outpatient clinics." *Obstetrics & Gynecology* 112 (2008): 891–98.

Huegel, Kelly. *GLBTQ: The Survival Guide for Queer and Questioning Teens.* Minneapolis: Free Spirit Publishing, 2003.

Langenberg, A. et al, "Development of clinically recognizable genital lesions among women previously identified as having 'asymptomatic' herpes simplex virus type 2 infection." *Annals of Internal Medicine* 110 (1989): 882–87.

Leridon, H. *Human Fertility: The Basic Components.* Chicago: University of Chicago Press, 1977.

Lisak, D. and Miller, P. M., "Repeat rape and multiple offending among undetected rapists." *Violence and Victim* 17(1) (2002): 73–84.

Lopez, Ralph I. *The Teen Health Book: A Parent's Guide to Adolescent Health and Well-Being.* New York: W. W. Norton & Company, 2003.

Mangione-Smith, R. et al, "Screening for chlamydia in adolescents and young women." *Archives of Pediatrics & Adolescent Medicine* 154 (2000): 1108–13.

Martin, E. T. et al, "A pooled analysis of the effect of condoms in preventing HSV-2 acquisition." *Archives of Internal Medicine* 169 (2009): 1233–40.

Mayle, Peter. *"What's Happening to Me?" A Guide to Puberty.* New York: Lyle Stuart, 2000.

McNeill, E.T. et al. *The Latex Condom: Recent Advances, Future Directions.* Research Triangle Park, NC: Family Health International, 1998.

McQuillan, G. M. et al, "Seroprevalence of human immunodeficiency virus in the US household population aged 18–49 years: the National Health and Nutrition Examination Surveys, 1999–2006." *Journal of Acquired Immune Deficiency Syndrome* 53 (2010): 117–23.

Medhus, Elisa. *Raising Children Who Think for Themselves.* Hillsboro, OR: Beyond Words Publishing, 2001.

National Research Council. *Understanding Violence Against Women.* Washington, D.C.: National Academy Press, 1996.

Saltzman. L. E. et al, "National Estimates of Sexual Violence Treated in

Emergency Departments." *Annals of Emergency Medicine* 49(2) (2007): 210–17.

Saracco, A. et al, "Man to woman sexual transmission of HIV: Longitudinal study of 343 steady partners of infected men." *Journal of Acquired Immune Deficiency Syndrome* 6 (1993): 497–502

Sedgh, G. et al, "Induced Abortion: Rates and Trends Worldwide," *Lancet*, 370 (2007): 1338–45.

U.S. Preventive Services Task Force. *Screening for chlamydial infection. In: Guide to clinical preventive services, an assessment of the effectiveness of 169 interventions.* Baltimore: Williams & Wilkins; 1989.

Weinstock, H. et al, "Sexually transmitted diseases among American youth: incidence and prevalence estimates, 2000." *Perspectives on Sexual and Reproductive Health* 36 (2004): 6–10.

White, E. et al, "Breast cancer among young US women in relation to oral contraceptive use." *Journal of the National Cancer Institute* 86 (1994): 505–514.

World Health Organization. *The Prevention and Management of Unsafe Abortion* (Geneva: WHO, 1992).

Xu, F. et al, "Trends in herpes simplex virus type 1 and type 2 seroprevalence in the United States." *JAMA* 296 (2006): 964–73.

ABOUT THE AUTHORS

Dr. Belisa Vranich is a clinical psychologist and media personality. She is the former advice columnist for New York City's *Daily News* and a current columnist for *The Huffington Post*. She is a regular guest on *Good Morning America*, *Today*, *Fox News*, and *Inside Edition*.

Holly Eagleson is the former features editor for *Cosmopolitan* and *Seventeen*, and has written for *Glamour*, *Everyday with Rachael Ray*, *New York Post*, and AOL's lemondrop.com.

Girlology...

A Girl's Guide to *Stuff that Matters*

Relationships, bodytalk & girl power!

Melisa Holmes, M.D.
&
Trish Hutchison, M.D.

Code 2955 • Paperback • $12.95

According to *Girlology*, knowledge is power—or more specifically—Girl Power! *Girlology* is for girls and about girls; it's not your typical sex-ed experience. It offers a powerful message based on helping girls get the facts, form their own opinions based on personal values, and apply these to everyday life.

The sequel to the mega-hit guide for girls Girlology, has become a brand, a culture that preteen and teen girls know and love and turn to for honest true-life advice on everything that matters most—friends, guys, body changes, dating, and sex. In *Girlology, Hang-Ups, Hook-Ups, and Holding Out*, girls will follow the true stories of four girls and their choices—good and bad.

Hang-Ups, Hook-Ups, and Holding Out

Stuff you need to know about your body, sex, and dating

"I said the 'L' word and he said nothing. Now what?"

"But I'm technically still a virgin, right?"

Melisa Holmes, M.D.
&
Trish Hutchison, M.D.
coauthors of Girlology

Code 5865 • Paperback • $14.95